clues to creativity

providing learning experiences
for children

Volume III

R - W

illustrations by Anne Gayler

M. Franklin and Maryann J. Dotts

friendship press ● new york

DEDICATION

To our parents,
for whom learning and discovery
have always
been
important.

Library of Congress Cataloging in Publication Data (Revised)
Dotts, M   Franklin, 1929-
   Clues to creativity.
   CONTENTS: v. 1. A-I.—   v. 3   R-Z.
   1. Creative activities and seat work. I. Dotts, Maryann J., joint
author. II. Title.
LB1537.D63   372.5   74-20622
ISBN 0-377-00015-9 (v. 1)

contents

preface

You are reading the third volume in a series of books containing *Clues to Creativity*. Volume 1 begins with a section entitled "Fostering Creativity in Children," which states our philosophy about creativity and how children learn. It shows our approach to the remainder of Volume 1, plus all of Volumes 2 and 3, which are a collection of suggestions for creative learning experiences for children. If you have not read that first part of Volume 1, we suggest you find it and read it.

The learning experiences (the remainder of Volume 1 and all of Volumes 2 and 3) are arranged alphabetically. Sections A through I are found in Volume 1, J through P in Volume 2, and the remainder of the alphabet in this volume. (See the back of this book for a list of contents of Volumes 1 and 2.)

You can use this book as you would an encyclopedia or the Yellow Pages in your telephone directory. If you want to know how children can enjoy *Weaving,* look up that heading in the contents and turn to the proper section in this book. The same is true for *Rhythm Instruments, Storytelling* or *Time Lines*—or any of the other headings in Volume 3.

We have tried to make the sections practical. They contain the basics you need to get started with each learning experience, rather than a lot of theory (we put that in "Fostering Creativity in Children" at the beginning of Volume 1!). We hope you will find here a practical set of clues you can use to increase creativity in learning experiences with children.

Who Can Use This Book

This book is especially for adults who work with children in the church. Some activities may be used with children as young as 4 or 5; younger ages are

4

usually specified where appropriate, or a special section may give a suggestion specifically for younger children. Older children will be able to do most all the things suggested here, as will junior highs. Some suggestions may even interest later teens.

This book might also be used by older children and youth themselves, either within an organized group or on their own. And parents may find some of these suggestions helpful as they try to provide opportunities for children to have creative experiences at home. In addition to informal use in the home, this book could also be used by family groups meeting together in homes for fellowship and study.

How to Use This Book

Each alphabetical section is self-contained. Normally you will read at any one time just that section in which you are currently interested. Very few persons will read this book all the way through from front to back!

Because each section must stand on its own, repetition is necessary. You will notice this if you read several sections together. As much as possible, each section has the same format, which includes six parts: WHAT IT IS, WHEN TO USE IT, WHERE TO USE IT, WHY CHILDREN USE IT, WHAT CHILDREN NEED, HOW TO DO IT. Some sections also include: RECIPES, WHERE TO GET MORE HELP, CROSS REFERENCING.

The three volumes of this series include over one hundred alphabetical sections. In such a series, however, all possible learning activities cannot be included, so we have had to make some choices, based on certain criteria. In general, these criteria are:

—activities that children can do with a minimum of adult help;

—activities requiring a minimum or no purchase of pre-packaged commercial materials, tools, equipment;

—activities that emphasize creative use of ideas and materials, rather than copying or following set patterns;

—activities using materials that are easily accessible and as inexpensive as possible;

5

—activities that stress flexible use of materials, i.e. using the same thing in several different ways, and
—activities leading to some discovery the child makes about herself or himself, as well as about the world and other people.

The emphasis in this book is on learning experiences for *children*, rather than for *adults*. Yet adults need to learn how to help children learn creatively. So the instructions or suggestions given for adults are intended to enable the leader to open up such experiences for the child. While explicit instructions may sometimes be given for the leader, their intent is only to free the adult by providing adequate background.

One important caution must be stated here. *Always try it yourself first!* Do not use these suggestions for the first time with the children present. This may easily lead to frustration for children and leaders alike. Try out the idea yourself. Learn what the suggestions and instructions mean and what possibilities they open up. Learn what a particular medium will do. Find out just what materials and supplies you need in order to help children do it. And, most important, be sure you know *why* you are helping children try out this kind of learning activity. By experimenting beforehand, you will be able to vary the suggestions and make them fit your own situation.

One other word of advice: this series of books is not a substitute for regular session planning or curriculum resources. When used with children's groups, these books should complement session plans and curriculum materials. The many learning experiences suggested here may be used to supplement and enrich the ideas you will develop as you do your own session planning and as you use your own curriculum resources.

To the Adult Who Uses This Book

You are a special person, as is each child with whom you work. You have your own creativity and your own desire to explore and experiment—to discover your own freedom. The purpose of this book is to give you ideas and try-out experiences so that you will be

6

free to let children experiment and explore on their own. Let the children do it! Give them a minimum of adult help so that they can experience maximum learning. Trust children and their own growth processes to develop their creativity.

We hope the suggestions in this series will help you and the children with whom you work to have many creative learning experiences.

M. Franklin Dotts
Maryann J. Dotts

records

WHAT THEY ARE—

Records are audio recordings preserved on flat plastic disks. The chief distinction between records and tapes is that records require an additional step—the transfer of recorded material from magnetic tape to the flat disk.

Children will probably use already-prepared records, while with tape they can make their own recordings or use those prepared by others.

WHEN TO USE THEM—

Children can use records whenever they need prerecorded sound, in either a formal or informal setting. If the children are learning a new and unfamiliar hymn or song, for example, they could use a record with the music recorded in such a form that it can be learned easily. If a story that would help to illustrate a particular emphasis is available on a record, use the record to share the story.

WHERE TO USE THEM—

Records can be used wherever a record player or phonograph is available. Some record players are battery-powered, but most require an electric power source. Some record players are equipped with a jack for a headset or earplug, so that individual children (or several if a multi-jack listening station is available) can use records without disturbing others nearby.

WHY CHILDREN USE THEM—

Records allow children to:
—hear a wide variety of prerecorded sounds, either individually or in groups
—learn and use music with recorded assistance

—make use of recorded stories and games
—appreciate the beauty of various kinds of music and stories.

WHAT CHILDREN NEED—

—a three-speed record player (young children need a very simple player that allows them to place the needle manually at the edge of the record and that has one simple volume control)
—records (begin to build a collection of records appropriate to the age group, subject areas and concerns of your group)
—listings of good records:
in your curriculum resources
in record catalogs
in retail record shops
—earphones and/or headsets and listening centers for individual or small group use.

HOW TO USE THEM—

Record content must fit in with the purpose of children's activities in order to be useful. This means that both children and their adult leaders need to decide ahead of time whether a particular recording will help them achieve their purposes.

Records in Church School Curriculum Resources

Records—or *sound sheets* as they are sometimes called—are often included as an integral part of church school curriculum. Almost always, a leader's guide or teacher's manual gives specific suggestions for using the record, often with a number of options from which to choose. You and your boys and girls may think of additional ways these records can be used.

Sometimes these records are manufactured in a thin, flexible vinyl that must be very carefully used and stored, so they do not get bent and become unusable. Rigid vinyl records are usually stored in cardboard jackets. While the flexible records are less durable and were not meant for permanent use, they can often be stored and used again if treated carefully. Sometimes these are square in shape, sometimes round. Sometimes they are bound into a curriculum study book; sometimes they come in a packet of teaching materials. Many teachers store square records in a three-ring binder by punching out two holes near the corners to match two rings in the binder. Records can then be arranged according to subject or age group.

Note: Flexible vinyl records work best when placed on the turntable *on top of* a rigid vinyl record, held to it firmly with a small piece of masking tape.

Records provided in curriculum resources contain many varieties of information. Music often predominates, with suggestions for using the record to learn new hymns or as familiar music to sing along with. Keep in mind the following criteria as you and your children select recorded music for "sing along" use:

1. You need good clear reproduction of the tune with simple, easy-to-follow accompaniment and a melody line that is distinct and recognizable. The music should be played in a key that children can use easily.

2. If the music has a vocal part, the words must be clear, distinct, and sung in a voice that is easy to follow, with a simple, direct arrangement.

3. The words should be available in written form (on the record album jacket, in an accompanying booklet, or in the teacher's manual or leader's guide). Words provided should match with the stanzas recorded.

In addition to music, records in your church curriculum may include stories, poems, interviews, suggestions for role play, movement, drama, activities, sound tracks for short filmstrips. Follow the suggestions given for use or brainstorm with your children some additional ways these can be used.

Records from Other Sources

Content of commercially-available records varies widely. You should evaluate them carefully with your purposes in mind.

Contemporary music, for example, often has many important messages, besides providing pure enjoyment. Many current songs have deep philosophical and theological messages. Which would be understandable and/or enjoyable for your children? See current music magazines as well as daily newspapers for regular record reviews.

Because the amount of material produced commercially is vast, children's leaders must select and use wisely—and with purpose—from the many choices.

Your Purpose Is Important

Know why you are using a record. You might begin by combining a record with some other activity. For instance, young children often find a new freedom of movement when they fingerpaint to music. Or music can be used as a background for story reading or as an inducement to read a particular story. Recorded music can provide a change of pace—as an active game, for instance, when young children have been still too long.

Certain records can help to foster imaginative development. Use such suggestions as: How do you feel when you hear that sound? What animal does this music suggest? Make your body move the way this music makes you feel.

When studying another culture, children can appreciate recordings of music and song from that part of the world. Sound effects records can heighten the realism of a story or play. Contemporary religious songs can easily be learned by using recordings, especially if a song book is available with the words.

Choosing and Using a Record

Here are some steps to help you evaluate and use records:

1. Select a record in keeping with the purpose of the learning experience.
2. Listen to it first as an adult, asking yourself:
—what are the most important parts?
—what questions does it raise that I may have to deal with?
—what are the most important sections to use?
—what parts could be deleted if necessary?
3. Set the scene for the listeners by giving background information and suggesting particular things to look for.

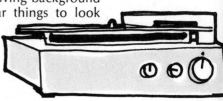

11

4. Listen to the recording with the group.
5. Share your feelings after hearing the record. Ask the children: What did it make you think of?
6. Listen to parts (or all) of the record again.
7. Evaluate together the record and your use of it.
8. Make use of this listening experience in further learning experiences of your group.

Individual and Small Group Use

Often listening to records or tapes can be an optional activity for individuals or small groups. In this case it is especially helpful if the phonograph is equipped with a mini phone jack for an earplug or headset so that children can listen individually.

Note: A jack can be installed on a record player at a reasonable cost at an electronic repair shop. Earplugs come in all price ranges, with the simplest between $1 and $2.

You can also purchase multiple-jack listening centers that enable a number of persons to listen to the same recording with earplugs.

You can make your own listening center:

LISTENING CENTER [1]
by Donn P. McGuirk

The listening center is a very helpful aid for small group or individualized instruction. All that is needed is an audio recorder (cassette or reel-to-reel) or a record player, either of which has a jack for a headset or external speaker, plus a distribution box with jacks for several headsets.

Although there are many excellent listening centers on the market, they are usually quite expensive. The one described below will accommodate from one to six earphones (or more if additional jacks are built into it). It can easily be assembled for under $10.00, including six of the earphones.

Through the use of the earphones, small groups of students can be involved in special assignments without disturbing other class activities.

---

[1] From CHURCH TEACHERS, Vol. 1, No. 2, September, 1973, Association of Church Teachers. Used by permission of the publishers.

RECORDS

MATERIALS:
- Fairly sturdy plastic refrigerator bowl with lid (4 or 5 inches in diameter)
- Six (or more) miniature 3.5 mm (approx. ⅛ inch) two-conductor, open-circuit, panel-mounting phone jack (Fig. 1.)*
- One standard, ¼ inch, two-conductor, open-circuit, panel-mounting phone jack (Fig. 2.)*
- Five feet single strand (solid) lightweight hook-up wire (size not critical, insulation not necessary)*
- One patch cable with a plug on one end to match the output jack on the recorder or record player, and a standard phone plug on the other*
- Six (or more) dynamic 8 ohm earphones with cord and miniature plugs (type used with transistor radios)*
- Pencil type soldering iron
- Resin core solder*
- Wire cutter

METHOD:
1. Make one hole (approx. ¼" in diameter) for each miniature jack on the side of the bowl, equi-distant from each other (Use either a, b, or c below.) (Fig. 3.)
a. Use the tip of the hot soldering iron to make the proper size hole. This will make quite an odor and some smoke (depending on the type of plastic). The tip of the iron should be wiped clean with an old rag immediately.
b. Drill the hole with a drill and ¼" bit. It may be possible to drill the hole by spinning the drill against the bowl with the fingers.
c. Cut the hole carefully with a small pointed blade.
2. Install the miniature jacks by pushing them from the inside of the bowl out through the holes and securing in place with the washers and nuts that come on the jacks. (Fig. 4.)
3. Install the larger jack making a ⅜ inch (approx.) hole in the top of the bowl and secure as described in #2, above. (Fig. 3.)
4. Connect all the jacks in parallel. In other words, connect a length of wire to lug Y of each jack, beginning with the larger one. Then connect a second length of wire to lug Z of each jack. (Fig. 4.)
5. Solder each connection carefully, making certain that enough heat is applied to allow the solder to flow around

---

*Available from radio supply stores and radio parts houses.

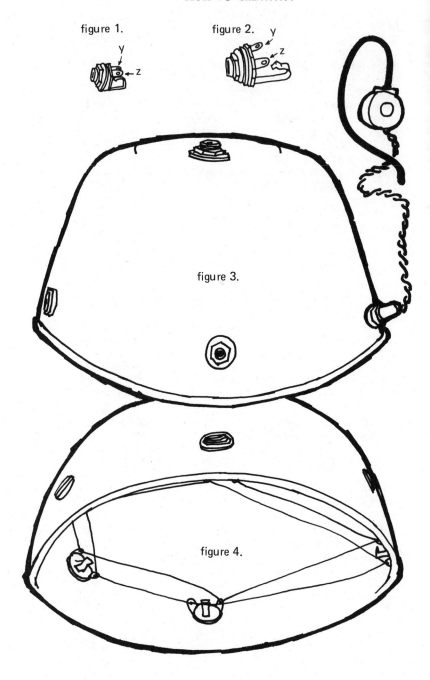

figure 1.

figure 2.

figure 3.

figure 4.

the wire and lug, but not so much heat that the bowl begins to melt. (This is the reason for using a small pencil type soldering iron.)

6. Arrange the wires so that they touch nothing but the lugs to which they are soldered. (*Fig. 4.*)

7. Use the listening center by plugging one end of the patch cable into the jack on the top of the bowl and the other end into the output jack of the recorder or record player. Then plug the desired number of earphones into the jacks on the side of the bowl, turn on the player, and adjust the volume. (*Fig. 3.*)

8. Store the earphones and patch cable in the bowl and cover it with the lid when not in use.

research

WHAT IT IS—

Research is the process of searching out information about a specific subject. The word *research* applies when children are asked to find facts or information and report to their group or put the material in some form that the group or individuals can use. Research is not an end in itself; the information will be used for some purpose.

WHEN AND WHERE TO DO IT—

Children do research when they look up a word in the dictionary, when they find out what kind of trees grow in another country or how Palestinian homes were built in Jesus' day, or when they compare prices while shopping for food for a picnic. Research is used by persons of elementary age and older when they need to find out something.

Children may need to go to many places to carry out their research—to libraries, stores, books, encyclopedias, to talk with certain persons (see Interview, Volume 1), to visit certain places (see Field Trips, Volume 1).

WHY CHILDREN DO IT—

Research allows children to:
—find answers to their questions
—collect information that will enable them to accomplish some other task, like writing a radio or TV script, answering a quiz, or understanding about a certain country
—discover information to share with others
—help their group by providing information for others as well as themselves.

WHAT CHILDREN NEED—

Note: specific resources needed will depend on the kind of information children are researching.
—some basic tools children can use:
an elementary dictionary
a Bible dictionary *(Young Readers Bible Dictionary* is a good one)
books about Christian symbols
Bible concordance (RSV)
Bibles in several modern translations
Atlas
Bible Atlas
books on specific subjects (on various reading levels) borrowed from libraries for classroom or home use

HOW TO DO IT—

1. *For Early Elementary Children.* A helpful aid to the child beginning to use research tools is a question clearly written on a card or piece of paper with a suggestion of a possible source. It even helps sometimes to have a book opened to a relevant passage. The child then may write a definition or explanation on another card or piece of paper. This information can be displayed or posted on the bulletin board so that the whole group has access to it. Use this kind of activity with vocabulary, key words or words the children might not know.

Obviously, early elementary children with beginning reading skills are limited to very simple research using the most elementary of sources. Find alternate ways for children to share their information—drawing pictures, telling what they found, talking into a tape recorder, making a display are possibilities.

2. *With Older Elementary Girls and Boys.* Older children can develop information cards about a variety of topics. Often they may need additional information in order to proceed on some other task. Research thus helps children accomplish another objective. It is one way of fulfilling our desire to know about many fascinating aspects of the world around us. Older elementary children will be able to do this in a much more systematic and organized way than younger children.

review

WHAT IT IS—

Review—a basic learning technique—is the process of going back over something that has already been learned. Much of our teaching and learning is such that one session or experience builds upon what has been learned previously. Thus, it is helpful to recall or repeat the previous experience or information by means of review. This also helps to ensure that the material is fully understood.

WHEN AND WHERE TO USE IT—

Children can use review techniques for summarizing at various steps along the way in any particular study, as well as at the end of a sequence or unit.

Review can be done in any place where children can go back over what they have already learned. Most often it is associated with regular classroom study and follows regular classroom learning activities.

WHY CHILDREN USE IT—

Review allows children to:
—refresh their memories on familiar learnings

—see new relationships among things they have learned
—integrate their new learnings with previous ones
—view what they have learned from a larger, broader perspective
—pull together and organize certain learnings in preparation for studying related or advanced areas.

WHAT CHILDREN NEED—

—creative suggestions for various ways to review
—adult leaders who make review activities an important part of their planning with children
—time and opportunity to help one another review
—motivation to review because of a desire to see new relationships, rather than because someone is going to give a test or ask some questions

HOW TO USE IT—

Teachers and children can use review in many ways.

A Pattern for Structuring a Class Session

Some teachers and their children plan a class session so that review is built in at each step:

Review (Make use of previous learning and information in new ways. Call to mind new associations; catch up those who were absent. Go deeper with some elements of the subject.)
New Material (Present new information or explain new material in an enthusiastic way.)
Laboratory (Students have opportunity to use the new information in practical situations, applying it, analyzing it, checking its usefulness in everyday living. The student should also use the new information outside the class session in actual situations.)

Some Common Elements in Review

Among the many ways to accomplish review, there are some common desirable elements:
1. Review activities should be fun. The activity should not be a dull repetition of what was done before, but a new approach with a new perspective.

2. Review activities should be self-directing, as much as possible. Develop games based on review information (such as relays, puzzles, working in categories, etc.). Develop review activities that the child can use alone, following instructions. Thus, each child can move at his or her own speed, spending more time on those things that need review the most.

3. Review activities should be as varied as possible. Find ways to review information dramatically (stories, plays, dramatizations, songs, poems, etc.). Use three-dimensional methods (charts, dioramas, displays, etc.).

4. Review activities should involve feelings as well as intellect (poems, stories and creative dramatics can be used).

5. Review activities should help build understanding of relationships (murals, mobiles, slides, sculpture, videotape, charts, posters, etc.).

A Suggestion

Refer to the sections mentioned above (see other sections in this series) for ways to adapt other activities for review purposes. For example, see Television, where a good review activity is suggested in the section entitled "Adapting Quiz Shows."

rhythm instruments

WHAT THEY ARE—

Rhythm instruments are manufactured and/or home-made objects that produce musical and rhythmic sounds. Children use them to accompany movement, singing, records, piano music or poetry that lends itself to rhythmic interpretation.

WHEN AND WHERE TO USE THEM—

Children use instruments when they want to produce rhythmic sounds for enjoyment, for experimentation, or because they are trying to learn about the music of a particular period, culture or type.

Children can use instruments inside or outside, individually or in groups. Most often children will use them in a group where they can create musical rhythms and sounds together.

WHY CHILDREN USE THEM—

Rhythm instruments allow children to:
—be involved with other children with some sound-producing tool, without being singled out for individual performances
—develop their natural sense of rhythm
—cooperate with other children to make musical sounds.

WHAT CHILDREN NEED—

—a wide variety of instruments (triangles and strikers, drums and drumsticks, wood blocks, tambourines, shakers or rattles, bells, sand blocks, rhythm sticks, cymbals, kazoos)
—music or records for the players to accompany
—materials and equipment for making instruments (see specific instructions below for materials)

HOW TO MAKE AND USE THEM—

Some instruments can be made by the children themselves. Large spikes with a yarn or string loop around the head can be struck with another nail. Wooden blocks can be made easily out of scrap wood. Experiment with different sizes and types of wood, and be sure the blocks are sanded and smooth before children use them. Pieces of dowel can be used to strike the wooden blocks.

You can make wooden blocks into sand blocks by covering them with sandpaper (rough side out) so that as the children rub them the paper makes a scratching sound. Sandpaper can be attached with thumbtacks.

Sleigh bells and jingle bells can be sewn to a piece of elastic to go around a child's wrist.

Tambourines can be made by lacing together two paper or aluminum plates and sewing bells around the edges with yarn. Shakers or rattles can be made with two aluminum pans from frozen meat pies. Lace together and place some dried beans or gravel inside for the rattle. Small plastic margarine tubs can be used for rattles, too, with dried beans inside and the plastic lid in place.

Drums can be made from a number of containers. One- or two-pound coffee cans usually come with plastic lids. Use the lid or stretch a piece of chamois over the top of the can. Oatmeal boxes are also suitable, as well as some plastic storage containers with lids. Experiment with the different sounds you can get. See *Steven Caney's Toy Book* by Steven Caney (see Bibliography) for a drum made from a wooden box.

To make a kazoo, cover the end of a cardboard tube with waxed paper and secure it with a rubber band. Punch a hole with a pencil about 1 inch in from the covered end. Hold the open end of the tube to your mouth and begin to hum. Use an "oo" or "doodoo" sound for another variety of sound. Two or three holes can be punched in longer tubes for a still different effect.

Help children explore many things around them and see what sounds they can make. Often metal racks, glasses and bottles will give many varieties of sounds.

role play

WHAT IT IS—

Role play is the spontaneous acting out of a situation, relationship, condition or circumstance through which the group seeks insight, especially as to how the characters portrayed might feel or how a problem can be solved. The players use pantomime and dialogue.

Role play will most often be used with older elementary children.

WHEN TO USE IT—

Role play is best used when an individual or a group needs to think through various alternative reactions to a situation, when a group is trying to find solutions to a problem, when a leader wants to give children opportunity to express opinions and gain insights into possible solutions.

Role play can be used in brief time periods, for the situations dramatized are not usually very long. It is important, however, to arrange for a de-roling time during which implications and insights can be clarified. If you do not have time for this discussion period, choose another activity instead of role playing.

WHERE TO USE IT—

Role play can be done in any location, since no equipment is needed. It is best if the children have had some previous experiences with movement (see Movement, Volume 2; Sensory Experiences).

WHY CHILDREN USE IT—

Role play allows children to:
—try on the role of another person
—explore possible ways to solve a problem
—feel at home with their own abilities to express themselves in a group
—realize that their own feelings, thoughts and actions are not necessarily unique
—create their own endings for open-ended stories.

WHAT CHILDREN NEED—

—opportunity to share feelings, understandings
—a leader who is sensitive to verbal and nonverbal signs individuals can give
—a climate in which children know they can explore a role play situation without embarrassment

HOW TO USE IT—

Role play can be carried out by following these steps:
1. *Establish the situation.* This includes the opening

of the story, scene, time and characters.

2. *Accept role assignments.* Players should volunteer, if at all possible. The rest of the group takes the role of viewers and discussion participants.

3. *Play the scene.* Do the scene. The leader should end the scene while the action is still going strong.

4. *De-role the players.* Announce that the players are now back to being themselves. Use their own names so that they do not carry their roles out into real life situations.

5. *Discussion.* The viewers and players talk together about the experience. What new insights did you receive from the role play? Try to analyze the understandings and role each person was portraying. How (through mannerisms, use of voice, physical movements, etc.) did the players help you understand the characters being played? What did you like about the action of the player(s)? What were some unspoken thoughts of the character you were portraying? How did you find yourself relating to the other characters?

6. *Further suggestions.* The discussion may result in new insights or suggestions for further playing. The scene could be played again, using another set of circumstances or feelings.

Note: No overall conclusions are arrived at through role play. Thinking continues and insights are developed even after the discussion is over. Because they can observe and be involved in the discussion, children who do not take active parts in the dramatization itself can still benefit from role play.

Ideas for the Leader

When selecting materials for role play, choose situations familiar to the children, such as family settings, conflict of interest situations, situations where personal feelings are involved.

Role play can be used as a review technique, bringing together information previously studied. For example, after studying the Joseph story in the Old Testament, the group might role play Joseph's feelings for his brothers in the various settings of the story.

rubbings

WHAT THEY ARE—

Rubbings are the designs achieved when thin paper is placed over a textured surface and rubbed or stroked.

Rubbings can be an exciting discovery process, revealing facets of everyday items that are not usually observed. Young children enjoy the almost magic experience of having the design appear when an object is rubbed. Many household and outdoor items can provide interesting raised designs. Older children can combine various textures to create abstract designs after they have experimented with the many surfaces around them.

In Thailand, making rubbings of the reliefs in the temples has become an art. The raised portion of the design is imprinted in crayon on paper, some in one color and others in several colors.

Children enjoy a rubbing because of its element of surprise. No one can be sure what the imprint will look like. This activity helps children develop their powers of observation—a rubbing encourages the viewer to look more closely at a design, since sometimes the details are not obvious as, for example, in the veins in a leaf.

Certain art forms can be collected through rubbings —for example, old tombstone inscriptions and low relief art, names and footprints in cement and metal castings as in historical markers. Such rubbings can be mounted and hung as art prints.

WHEN TO MAKE THEM—

Children can make rubbings any time they have a reason to reproduce on paper the image of a raised surface. This might be when they are studying a particular subject and find appropriate designs. Or it

24

might be when children simply want to create interesting designs and patterns.

WHERE TO MAKE THEM—

Depending on the portability of the object to be rubbed, children may have to do their rubbings in specific places. Inscriptions on buildings, markers and sidewalks will obviously have to be rubbed wherever they are, while coins, stones and pieces of wood can be moved to a convenient location for rubbing.

WHY CHILDREN MAKE THEM—

Rubbings allow children to:
—become aware in a new way of certain surface textures
—reproduce in their own way a particular design
—combine rubbings of several different surfaces to make a pleasing design
—discover unexpected beauty in everyday surfaces
—experiment with different color combinations.

WHAT CHILDREN NEED—

—thin paper (onionskin, typing paper, duplicating paper)
—crayons, soft lead pencils (#2), china marker
—textured objects (cardboard, corrugated cardboard, wallpaper, leather, walls, stair treads, grasses, leaves, wood, bark, pegboard, cork, etc.)
—household items (kitchen tools, including turners, spatulas, measuring spoons, forks; bottle tops; place mats; textured glasses; keys, coins; coat hangers; cane chair seats; combs; spiral binders of a book)
—low-relief art objects, like symbols in mosaics
—other textured objects

HOW TO MAKE THEM—

Young children enjoy rubbing the side of a crayon over a comb, and seeing all the short straight lines appear. Little assistance is needed once the children get the idea of placing the paper on top of the items and rubbing with the crayon.

Older children will first experiment to see what designs are made by certain items. Then they will begin to place those shapes in patterns to create designs of their own. Allow them to experiment, and to use their imaginations.

1. *Multiple copies.* Children can use the rubbing process to make many copies of the same design for booklet covers, invitations, announcements, etc. The object to be rubbed, such as a design cut out of corrugated cardboard, would be mounted on a larger sheet of cardboard. Then children can rub as many copies as are needed.

2. *Candle Resist.* Rub a candle over the textured surface on paper. Then apply a wash of water color or tempera. As in any crayon resist, the color will not take on the wax design. This process reproduces the textured pattern in still another way.

WHERE TO GET MORE HELP—

Seidelman, James E. and Grace Mintonye, *The Rub Book.* New York: Macmillan, 1968. $3.50.

Sculpture

Sculpture is the art of creating three-dimensional figures and designs by carving, casting, shaping or modeling. The original meaning of the word *sculpture* is *to cut,* but the art now includes all of the following processes: (1) cutting or carving figures or designs from blocks of some substance like wood or stone; (2) casting figures or designs in a permanent material like bronze from a mold; and (3) modeling a figure or design in some pliable material like clay, wax, paper, or wire.

See the following sections for complete discussions of various forms of sculpture as used with children: in **Volume 1,** Carving, Casting, Clay Modeling; in **Volume 2,** Paper (Paper Sculpture); in this volume, Wire Sculpture.

Sensory experiences

WHAT THEY ARE—

We include here learning experiences especially designed to foster use of the senses of sight, smell, touch and hearing. Such experiences increase children's alertness to the world around them and are the basic means through which children learn.

Probably all the learning experiences suggested in this book make use of one or more of the senses. But by calling particular attention to certain experiences here, we hope to heighten your sensitivity to the need among children to use all the senses.

WHEN TO HAVE THEM—

There is almost no limit to the opportunities for children to become more aware of the world around them through sensory experiences. These can be brief, momentary experiences, planned or unplanned. They can stand alone, or they may be tied in with other experiences. They can occur when a class is meeting or when a child is learning on his or her own.

WHERE TO HAVE THEM—

The kinds of sensory experiences described here can happen in many places. Some must be planned for a place where certain equipment is available. Others will occur in connection with a particular unplanned sensory event, like the song of a particular bird or the smell of pine needles in the forest. Thus, certain sensory experiences will occur in the organized classroom setting while others will occur in many places beyond the classroom.

WHY CHILDREN HAVE THEM—

Sensory experiences allow children to:
—enlarge their understanding of the world

—become more and more alert to the world around them
—enjoy many sensory experiences and see relationships among them; sense and enjoy the order of God's world
—gain an increasing appreciation of their own abilities
—appreciate and enjoy the multi-sensory nature of many learning experiences.

WHAT CHILDREN NEED—

—tape recorder (to record sounds during a quiet listening period)
—tray of six to twelve familiar items for quick looking experiences—a crayon, a penny, a hair barrette, a safety pin, a pair of scissors, a small ball, etc.
—blindfolds
—food items for tasting, such as candy, popcorn, celery, etc.
—items to smell, such as chewing gum, mint candy, peanut butter cookies, shaving lotion, soap
—liquid soap, water, bowl, wire whisk or rotary egg beater
—white soap flakes, tree branches, finger paint paper or shelf paper

HOW TO HAVE THEM—

As children grow older, they learn to use their senses more and more efficiently. Often, however, we use our sight and our hearing more than the other senses. Sometimes leaders and teachers miss opportunities to provide children with learning experiences that make use of more than one sense.

Suggestions given below will heighten your own sensitivity to the possibilities for sensory learning experiences. You should very quickly be able to go far beyond these few simple suggestions to find additional activities you can use constantly.

Feeling Me with Me!

We rarely think about our own bodies and how they feel. We don't think about our feet until a shoe hurts or rubs a blister. Each of us needs to stop and realize how it feels to be ourselves! Here is an exercise you can do yourself. Staying right where you are, take in every part of yourself as if you were meeting that part for the first time.

Start at the bottom. Is your foot in a shoe or is it bare, touching the floor or the grass or the sidewalk? What does it feel like? Do you have socks on? How do they feel? Is it warm in your shoe? Smooth? Rough? Wet? How does the floor feel beneath your feet? Solid, weak, shaky, smooth? How do your toes feel?

Move on to your ankle and discover what is happening there, and then to the knee, waist, chest, neck, arms and head. Think of all the feelings you experience as each part relates to the others and to the world around it.

Now think of ways you can help your children begin to sense how their bodies feel. You might want to talk just about the feet in one session and do the head at another, the arms and hands at still another.

Ask older children to feel the parts of their bodies without actually touching them with their hands. Help them learn to concentrate and use their feeling within that portion of their bodies.

Listen to the World Around You

Have an individual or the group sit quietly for one minute and listen to the sounds close around them. In any setting we screen out certain sounds so that they do not bother us. After the minute is up have the children compare by telling what sounds they heard. You may want to make a list. Which sound was the most pleasant? Most exciting? Which was most unpleasant or frightening? If you have a tape recorder, you might make a recording during the one minute of silence, then play it back to verify what various people report they heard.

A Quick Look

Gather together on a tray items familiar to the children—about six items for young children and twelve or more for older children. Allow them to look at the objects for ten to fifteen seconds and then cover the tray. Ask young children to tell what they saw,

29

describing the items as fully as they can. Ask elementary children to write down on a list as many of the items as they can recall. When all have finished, tally up the number of items viewed. You might ask someone to describe a specific item, such as a wallet with leather tooling on it. Did most people see the details or just the wallet? When all questions have been answered and ideas compared, look at the tray again. Read off the items and have children check their lists. Did anyone remember everything? Did anyone write down something that was not on the tray?

Tasting

Provide blindfolds or ask children to close their eyes. Then give each a piece of food on their tongue —candy, popcorn, celery, etc. Use foods with different textures, shapes and flavors. Ask the children to feel the food in their mouths and begin to get some idea about its flavor, color, shape, etc. Talk about each food after children have had time to decide what each one is. Then look at it. Was the person right? What was the best clue for knowing what it was?

Smelling

With eyes blindfolded or closed, children are given a chance to smell such items as a piece of clove-flavored chewing gum, mint candy, peanut butter cookies, shaving lotion, soap. Ask the children to identify the objects, giving their reasons, and then see if their decisions were accurate. Ask them to explain what clues they received through their sense of smell. Talk about some objects that have the same smell but are very different, such as pine needles and a pine-scented candle.

Fun with Soap

Children can explore soap in many forms as sensory experiences, especially experiences of touch. Children should be allowed to explore and experiment with many kinds of soaps.

For young children, discovery of the various properties of soap is important. Explorations may take place in a home living center in a classroom, or in the bathtub at home. Mix a few drops of liquid soap with a half cup of water in a bowl, whipping with a wire whisk or rotary egg beater until you have suds. Now measure the liquid. How much do you have? How much did you start with? Let these suds sit for a while or overnight. Now how much liquid do you have? Do you still have suds? Where did they go?

Children can decorate with whipped soap. Whip one cup of white soap flakes (not granules) with one-half cup of water until they peak like egg whites and then decorate tree branches. With the fingers, put tufts of "snow" onto the branches. Children can also do soap painting, which is similar to finger painting, except that whipped soap is used in place of finger paint. Be sure to dampen the finger paint (or shelf) paper before the children apply the whipped soap.

WHERE TO GET MORE HELP—

Tobey, Kathrene M., *Learning and Teaching Through the Senses*. Philadelphia: Westminster Press, 1970. $2.45 (paper).

Sewing

WHAT IT IS—

In this section we will assume that children have explored various kinds of stitches through weaving and stitchery (see Weaving and Stitchery) and are now ready to make a complete cloth or leather item.

Sewing is most appropriate for older elementary children, since it involves a number of skills younger children may not yet have.

WHEN TO DO IT—

Older children will sew when they want to make cloth items to wear or use. Sometimes these items

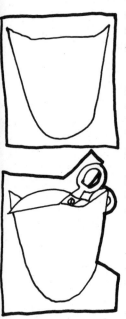

will be an end in themselves, but at other times children will use the sewing process to complete some other project that calls for items you can make.

WHERE TO DO IT—

Simple sewing does not take a lot of equipment or space, so children should be able to do it almost anywhere. If the use of the sewing machine is to be taught, instruction will need to be careful and detailed, and certain equipment will be necessary. Such groups as an older elementary interest group from a community center, a 4-H or Scout group could progress into machine sewing after studying the more simple techniques.

WHY CHILDREN DO IT—

Sewing allows children to:
—make useful items
—explore the properties of cloth and leather
—experience a procedure that requires a certain sequence of steps
—learn to use a pattern
—work out their own ideas for creating items.

WHAT CHILDREN NEED—

—various kinds of fabric (use a variety of materials in keeping with the particular project being undertaken)
—needles (both sharp needles and tapestry needles)
—needle threader
—threads appropriate to the fabric being used
—sharp cloth scissors
—iron for pressing
—commercial patterns, if clothing is to be made
—shredded foam, nylon hose, fabric scraps (for stuffing)

HOW TO DO IT—

Most children will use this kind of sequence for the projects they undertake:

1. Decide what to make and choose appropriate fabric and thread.

2. Get a pattern. Sometimes children will make their

own patterns out of large pieces of paper. Let them draw the shapes themselves on their pattern paper; be sure they have left adequate space around the edges for their seams. As they plan the size of the item, children should decide where any openings and folds will be. When children use commercially prepared patterns, they will need to read the pattern accurately, after instruction. Careful work at this point will prepare for the cutting step.

3. Cut out the fabric. With the pattern pieces pinned in place, the children should carefully cut the fabric. Be sure that two identical pieces are cut where necessary.

4. With right sides of material together, sew along seams. At this point zippers, if used, should be installed.

5. Turn the material right side out.

6. Sew any hooks and eyes, snaps or pull cords, etc.

7. Press the item with an iron.

Some Ideas for Sewing Projects

Here are some sewing projects that children can tackle:

Toys: stuffed toys, animals and shapes,
    catnip toys (small lightweight toys for pet cats, stuffed with nylon stockings and catnip)

Pet Collars: ribbon or felt decorated for the holidays; a large snap can be used to close it

Bags: tote bags or purses, treasure or toy bags (the drawstring type is easiest)

Clothing: poncho, headbands, belts, peasant blouses or dresses, boleros or vests

Pillows: squares or other shapes; close with a zipper

Doll Clothes: See Dolls, Volume 1.

Two Sewing Projects

1. *Carry-all Bag.* To make a bag that can carry many things to many places, cut two pieces of denim (jean-type fabric) 18 x 12 inches (or, if you have it, fold one piece 18 x 24 inches to the 18 x 12-inch size). Fold over one 18-inch edge about ½ inch deep and then fold again, creating a ½-inch seam across what will be the opening of the bag. Sew this seam securely. Do

this seam on the second piece of material as well. Place the two pieces with right sides together and sew down one side, across the bottom and up the other side. Turn this right side out and the seamed edges should be at the top. Note that if you began with the 18 x 24-inch piece of material you will only have to sew up both sides, since the bottom will be the folded side. For carrying straps or handles, cut two pieces of material 24 x 3 inches. Fold each strap lengthwise with right side in and sew down the open side. Turn it right side out by attaching a safety pin to one end and pushing the pin through the inside. After both straps are made, decide where to place them and sew them securely by hand to the inside top edge of the bag. This completes the bag, except for any decorating the children may want to do.

2. *Pillow.* Draw a design for a pillow on two pieces of material, making sure that both are the same size and shape. Almost any shape will work, but let's use a butterfly as an example. When you draw the design be sure to add an extra inch all the way around for a sewing seam. One piece of material can be decorated as the children wish. With right sides of the material together, sew all the way around except for a 4-inch opening. Turn the pillow cover inside out through the 4-inch opening, so the right side is out. Stuff with shredded foam, nylon hose, scraps of material or whatever else you have. Sew up the remaining four inches to complete the pillow.

Simulations

WHAT THEY ARE—

A simulation is the use of a certain social situation and a controlled set of factors, structures, and relationships with a certain number of players, in such a way that the players have an opportunity to see how they function individually and/or in groups within that kind of situation. Many simulations involve role play, with players taking on roles of certain individuals or group members in the specified setting in order to understand better what is happening to such persons. An essential part of the simulation is the discussion that follows the actual playing. Participants evaluate what has happened to the players, how they felt and now feel, and what the consequences of their actions and decisions were. This understanding of simulations excludes all other kinds of games (see Games, Volume 1).

True simulations are probably most appropriate at the upper elementary levels, although certain activities can help younger children get ready for the experience of using simulations. For example, children below first grade can use pantomime and creative play to build a pretend environment. Children begin at an early age in their play to think of themselves as other persons. They devote much energy to playing the role of another person. This is valuable preparation for later use of simulations. Use fairly simple simulations with children, reserving more detailed and involved simulations for teenagers and adults.

WHEN TO USE THEM—

Simulations are teaching tools and should be used to help children experience the area of study they are dealing with. Use simulations with children to provide a real-life setting in which to duplicate in miniature some problems and decisions related to the subject they are studying. Simulations often compress a long time span into a few "rounds of play," and children are better able to deal with various situations as they are presented. They can also see the results of their decisions. As children take on the roles of other persons they begin to understand some of the elements and consequences in real-life decisions.

Simulations take varying lengths of time. Some can be continued from one play session to another; others must be completed in a single block of time. Some require only a small amount of time; others require much more. Directions must be followed carefully. All these factors should be taken into account when choosing simulations to use with children in certain settings.

WHERE TO USE THEM—

Simulations can be used wherever there is space to develop the kinds of playing areas the instructions call for.

WHY CHILDREN USE THEM—

Simulations allow children to:
—take adult roles in a lifelike but controlled setting
—begin to learn how groups, organizations and companies function under certain conditions
—understand some factors that help events happen the way they do
—get practice in making decisions and following through to see the results.

WHAT CHILDREN NEED—

—To develop your own simulations, use a book like *Gaming* by Dennis Benson (see Bibliography for this and other books on simulations).
—To use commercially prepared simulations, purchase or borrow carefully chosen ones. Become thoroughly familiar with the purpose, rules and procedures. Be certain that the one you choose contributes to the goals you are trying to reach with children.

HOW TO USE THEM—

The three main steps in using a simulation are preparation, playing and post-play activity. Let's take a look at each step.

Preparation. This step involves creating or obtaining a simulation that will achieve your group's goals. The leader must get acquainted with the rules and collect any necessary materials. Plan to "walk through" the simulation with a small group, if possible. Write out ahead of time some evaluation or debriefing questions for the post-play period. Remember that these questions should bring into focus what the players have experienced.

Playing. This is the time the group actually spends

going through the simulation. As a leader, you may direct the playing; or perhaps one of the children can become familiar with the instructions and lead the group through the simulation. Read the instructions carefully for clues as to the kind of leadership needed while the simulation is going on.

Post-play Activity. This third step is often called debriefing or, in some cases, de-roling. After the period of play has ended, it is important to announce clearly that the simulation is *over.* Participants should know precisely when they are giving up their roles (if they have been playing roles) and when they are beginning to look at what they have just experienced. At this point you as director (or a child leader) will use the evaluation questions.

This third step—the evaluation of the learnings achieved during play—distinguishes simulations from other games. Here are some areas to consider during this evaluation period:

How did the simulation compare with the real world as you know it?

How did you feel about the role you were playing? About others on the opposite team?

Did you use any new skills during this simulation? What strategies did your team or group plan to use to solve its task in the simulation? Were these the best strategies or would you recommend others now? Would you want to play the simulation again?

What would you change if you were to play it again? Be sure to read the instructions carefully to see if they suggest any other specific questions that can be used during this post-play period.

Try This Common Format

Here is a common simulation format that you can develop to fit any particular subject area:

RATE IT—Register *AT*titudes and *E*xperiences

Use this technique to get at individuals' feelings about many topics—the menu for a picnic, value judgments on an open-ended story, a class vote on likes and dislikes. This simulation does not involve role playing.

Step 1. Preparation. Make an actual or imaginary

line down the middle of the room. One end of the line is for "like" or "agree," and the other end is for "dislike" or "disagree." At several intervals along this line mark off spots for "like a little bit," "it's all right," and "dislike some."

When a statement is read, each person decides how he or she feels about it, then stands along the line at the point closest to his/her feeling. Examples of questions: How do you feel about sour apples? How do you like blueberry muffins? Obviously sour apples may have most people near the "dislike" end, while blueberry muffins may have people spread along the line at a number of places.

With categories ranging from "Agree" to "Disagree," children might respond to statements like:
All mothers are happy.
Children want to ride in airplanes.
Fathers can ride bicycles.
Books have interesting stories.
All Chinese people come from China.

Make up your own statements and mark off the line on the floor (or in the grass if you are playing outside). Also make up post-play questions: How did you feel when you agreed with everyone else? When you were different from all the rest? What items did most people agree on? What items did most disagree on? What other words, phrases, statements or questions would you have included?

Step 2. Playing. Play the RATE IT game with the statements or words you have developed.

Step 3. Post-play Activity. Talk together about your experiences, using the questions you planned.

This simulation is a simple attempt to help children realize the difficulty of getting a group of people to agree on something. It also illustrates how some issues require more agreement than others, and deals with individual and group feelings and values.

A World Hunger Simulation

A simple simulation will illustrate for children something of our world's population and hunger problems. For advance preparation, the leader should look up current population figures for each continent in an encyclopedia or information almanac. As play begins, designate seven areas of the floor according to the continents—Asia, Africa, Australia, Europe, North America, South America, Antarctica.

Tape sheets of newsprint together to form a "tablecloth" for each continent. Divide the children into seven equal-sized groups, and ask each group to decorate a tablecloth (using felt markers or crayons) as beautifully as possible.

When all the tablecloths are completed and displayed on the floor, provide each group with a basket of fruit (including one of each kind) and one doughnut. Then redivide the children according to population, with the smallest number in Antarctica and the largest number in Asia.

Invite the children to sit down and eat their meal. It will soon become evident that some of the world's people do not have sufficient food for their numbers; others have more than they need.

At this point the "playing" is stopped, and post-play activity begins. Distribute extra food to the groups not having enough, so that all members can share the meal. In the post-play evaluation, discuss your feelings when you did not have enough food or when you had too much. Help children share their understandings of our need to be more concerned about the distribution of food to all the people of the world.

WHERE TO GET MORE HELP—

Schrank, Jeffrey, *Using Games in Religion Class.* Paramus, N.J.: Paulist Press, 1973. 23 pp. 35¢.

slides

WHAT THEY ARE—

A slide is a still photograph or drawing prepared on 35mm film for projection and mounted separately in a slide mounting. Since the 2 by 2-inch slide and projection equipment are now so common, we will discuss only slides in the 2 by 2-inch format.

WHEN TO MAKE AND USE THEM—

Slides help children to visualize something through projected pictures. This could be when they want to keep a record of some experience or activity (like a field trip) or when they want to illustrate through projected pictures a story, scenes from a particular country, the way people dress, or the kinds of homes persons have in various countries. Children can also communicate by making their own slides.

WHERE TO MAKE AND USE THEM—

Slides can be projected almost anywhere indoors—on a screen, wall or white sheet in a darkened room. Or, for a small group, they can be projected into a small table-top screen made out of a cardboard carton that has had its (inside) bottom covered with white paper and has been turned on its side.

Small hand viewers can also be used by individuals or small groups. These can either be electrically lighted or held up to a natural light source. With a slide sorter you can view twenty to thirty slides at one time, but without magnification. If a projector is used, you will, of course, need an electric power source.

WHY CHILDREN MAKE AND USE THEM—

Slides allow children to:
—view pictures in a sequence they themselves select
—make a choice from among a large number of pictures, using those most appropriate to their purposes
—combine a visual input with some accompanying verbal information
—create their own messages and designs by preparing their own slides
—plan their own visual presentations
—make a permanent record of important experiences.

WHAT CHILDREN NEED—

Following is a description of various types of slides and slide mounts. Lists of materials needed for specific projects will be given below, along with instructions.

There are four different types of 2 by 2-inch slides, according to the size of the opening in the center of the slide (see illustrations, p. 45).

a. The regular slide mount for 35mm film is used in processing most color slides. Ready-mount slide mountings also come in this size. The opening measures 1⅜ by 15/16 inches.

b. Slides made from Instamatic 126 cartridge cameras produce slides with an opening 1 1/16-inch square.

c. Super slide mounts may be purchased and are supplied in some class teaching packets. These can also be made from index card stock or poster board. The opening measures 1½ by 1½ inches. These can be sealed with rubber cement or taped around the outside edges with dark ⅜-inch cloth mending tape or slide binding tape.

d. Half-frame mounts are available for recycling commercial filmstrips into slides. The opening measures 15/16 by 11/16 inches.

To be sure you are getting the proper slide mounts, take the film to be used to an audiovisual dealer or camera supply store. A good dealer will be able to help you. Note that most cardboard slide mounts are inexpensive and are often sold in boxes of one hundred.

Most commercial cardboard mounts can be sealed with a warm iron (to join the two halves) or have a glued surface that can be sealed with a slightly wet artist's brush.

One-piece plastic mounts with an opening into which film slips are reusable and require no adhesive. Even more permanent is a metal slide mount that holds the film between two pieces of glass to protect it from fingerprints. Art prints or good purchased slides are safest in these mounts.

HOW TO MAKE AND USE THEM—

Identifying the Slides

If you place an identifying mark in one corner of each slide, you can eliminate upside down and backwards showings. Put a dot of ink, an adhesive dot, or any other marking you choose on the mounted slide in the lower left corner when you are looking at the picture with its subject matter right side up and left to right. When you are ready to project, rotate the slide so that the spot is in the upper right corner, and make sure that all the spots are in a row.

To put captions or other identifying words on the slides, use a permanent pen on cardboard frames and pressure-sensitive stickers on metal and plastic frames.

Before Making Slides

Use some preparatory activities with children before they begin to make slides. Making slides is most useful when children have explored a story, an event, a topic, or a culture and want to bring their thoughts together to share with others. This may be in the form of a word, like *caring*, or a concept, like *ecology*. It may be a story of our church, symbols, seasons, our activities, our world, etc.

When the group has done some thinking about the subject, they will have many ideas and will need to begin focusing on which are the most important, deciding which can best be shown in slides and which can best be done in other ways. Slides should be only one of several options available.

Ways to Make Slides

1. *Slides with a "No Flash Camera."* To produce a slide of a particular picture, take a colored slide picture outdoors with your camera. Put the picture to be reproduced flat on the ground or rest it against a plain background in a sunlighted area. If the camera is adjustable, set the distance; if it is a fixed focus camera, measure out a distance of 3 to 4 feet. Stand over or in front of the picture so that your body does not cast a shadow on it. Frame the picture in the viewfinder, snap the photo, and then have your color film developed. Use this process when you need slides of certain places, people, pictures, but have only flat pictures. Many excellent resources are available in magazines and picture files. Check at your camera shop for the best type of film to use for this job. (See Cameras, Volume 1, for equipment suggestions.)
2. *Color Slides Without a Camera.*
    a. Color Lifts: This is a process of lifting the printing

ink off a page so that it adheres to a piece of clear adhesive vinyl. To do color lifts children will need:
—transparent adhesive vinyl (available under several brand names)
—magazines, catalogs, newspapers, and other picture sources that can be cut up
—scissors
—water in cups or small dishes
—paper toweling
—slide mounting frames
—a warm iron to seal mounts
—felt pens for background color.

The success of color lifts varies with the type of ink and paper used in the picture source. To find a good source, try out several types of magazines and newspapers ahead of time. Cut the vinyl into a square slightly smaller than 2 x 2 inches and remove the backing. Place the vinyl onto a small picture or portion of a picture that you want to lift onto your slide. Be certain to smooth the air bubbles out as you place the vinyl on the paper. (Start from one side and let it down gently.) Rub the whole picture gently with the edge of a spoon, ballpoint pen cap, scissors handle or other hard smooth edge. This helps the ink adhere to the sticky side of the vinyl.

Now place the vinyl in a small cup of warm water for a few minutes. Rub the paper off the back of the vinyl and rinse several times. Remove all lint, leaving the ink from the picture on the vinyl surface. Let this dry in a spot where it will not pick up more lint. Then apply a second piece of vinyl, sealing the colored ink between the two layers. Arrange the vinyl in the slide mount frame and seal in place.

Some persons like to add background color with glass stain, felt markers, or Crystal Craze (trademark) paints. Experiment with ways of adding color before the second piece of vinyl is applied. Other things, like colored tissue, confetti, etc., can be used to make dark, bold shapes on the slide.

Note: Color lifts can be made in larger sizes for use in peep boxes, mobiles and as transparencies. Experiment to see what children will come up with.

b. Write-on Slides: To do write-on slides, children will need:

—blank slide material (this can include commercially prepared "blank" slides that have a matte acetate mounted in frames—one brand is Kodak Ektagraphic; heavy acetate such as is used for overhead transparencies in slide mounts; X-ray film that has been exposed, washed in bleach water, rinsed and mounted in slide mounts)

—writing tools (projection pencils, pencils, pens and markers, as used for transparencies, permanent felt pens, ballpoint pens, crayons, etc.). Try out whatever is available. Experiment with adding light background colors with glass stain, Crystal Craze (TM) and colored drawing inks like India ink.

Children can use write-on slides in numerous ways. For instance, when older elementary children have been working in committees and need to report to the total group, give them four or five blank slides and suggest that they write the key ideas for their presentation and then share with the rest of the group. Often a quick stick figure and/or a word will help get a message across effectively.

Experiment with different kinds of writing tools to see which work best under various conditions. Some marking tools do not yield dark solid colors when projected and require a darker room than others.

c. Recycling Used 35mm Film, Filmstrips and Slides: Look around for damaged filmstrips, film that has been developed and unwanted slides that did not turn out but are clear enough to use. Out-of-date or damaged filmstrips are a good picture source. Cut them apart and mount frames you can use in half-frame mounts. Decide the order in which you want to use them and delete outdated or unwanted frames. You can also use write-on slides to add questions, key words or ideas to provide smooth transitions.

Another possibility is to cut up the "leader" of an old filmstrip (this is usually black) and mount it in ready-mount frames. Using a sharp instrument (the end of a paper clip, knife point, scissors, etc.), on the dull (emulsion) side of the film, scratch in words or drawings to add another dimension to your pictures.

Also, old slides can be used with part of the picture blacked out with tape or colored with glass stain.

TYPES OF SLIDES

A. Regular slide mount

B. Instamatic 126 cartridge

C. Super slide mount

D. half-frame mount

Prepared Teaching Slides

A projected picture can quickly focus everyone's attention. Worship moments or meditations can be built around one picture. Discussions can be sparked by a single picture. Choose your pictures carefully and allow the children to express their reactions.

Often prepared art slides come with a script. Don't let a prepared script stifle you! Work out your own for your particular group. With children, you might show just one picture and talk about it. Or use a series of slides and let the children create their own story to go with the pictures. Use a tape recorder if you wish to "capture" such spontaneous stories.

Remember Always: Use only as many pictures as you really need to get across your message or accomplish your purpose!

Organizing Slides

An inexpensive slide sorter is helpful for gathering together a group of slides in proper order. The sorter is a collapsible plastic panel with ridges and a light bulb behind it, so arranged that you can see twenty to thirty slides at one time in several straight rows. Once the slides are arranged, you can transfer them to a cartridge or box in preparation for showing. Slide sorters are available at camera stores.

Small groups can also use the sorter for viewing if magnification is not required. Ten to fifteen slides can remind a class of their summer experiences, advertise a summer camping program, visualize a season or a place.

Preparing a Script

Older elementary students can work out a dialogue, a scenario or a script for a series of slides. Younger children can talk spontaneously about each picture. Encourage both approaches, depending on the age of your group.

Try to limit the script to about two sentences for each slide. Use the slide sorter to help children organize the pictures.

If the group wants to record their script, write it out first and have a reader practice ahead of time so that the tape recording allows time to project the slides. One way to help children pace their pauses between slides would be to have them count slowly to themselves, "One, two, three," before reading the script for the next picture.

Encourage older elementary children to plan their words carefully to tie in with the sequence of their slides. Encourage them to experiment with all kinds of slide presentations, as well as with scripts and sound tracks.

Soap

Soap Carving . . . . (see Carving, Volume 1)
Whipped Soap . . . . . . (see Sensory Experiences in this volume)

stabiles

WHAT THEY ARE—

A stabile is an arrangement of objects mounted on the end of pieces of wire, with all wires fixed in a solid base. Individual pieces have only a limited amount of movement, whereas in a mobile they may be moving constantly. Some of the same principles apply to both, however.

Younger children can attach items to pipe cleaners and secure them in a Styrofoam base. Older children can do more intricate experimenting to establish the exact amount of weight certain sized wires will hold so the object will move in the air currents.

WHEN AND WHERE TO MAKE THEM—

Children can make stabiles when they are interested in experimenting with the relative weights of a group of objects or when they wish to display a group of things in a new and different way.

Stabiles can be made in areas with limited space and resources and can be related to various seasons and subject matter.

WHY CHILDREN MAKE THEM—

Stabiles allow children to:
—experiment with the way objects move when mounted on wire
—discover pleasing relationships as they arrange objects
—bring together symbols or objects that relate to a particular historical period or person or country and arrange them in a three-dimensional, movable display
—experiment with concepts of weight and balance.

WHAT CHILDREN NEED—

—bases: These will vary according to purpose and what is available. Typical bases are:
Styrofoam packing pieces for lightweight items
plaster of Paris in flower pots, plastic margarine
tub, or lids of aerosol cans
pieces of wood, blocks, logs, limbs
—wire: stiff coat hanger wire
fine wire (1/16) for movement
5-64 spring steel wire
pipe cleaners
—nylon thread
—long-nosed pliers
—heavy scissors
—display objects:
seashells, bits of driftwood, seeds, dried flowers,
pretty small stones
—cupcake papers with flower seals
other pictures or objects appropriate to your subject
—plaster of Paris
—hand drill
—white glue, household glue

HOW TO MAKE THEM—

Making stabiles requires a lot of experimenting, because children must discover what will work before they can be sure how the pieces will fit together.

Patience is required, too, because you must wait for glue to dry or plaster of Paris to set. If the young artist is too anxious, the weight of the object on top of the wire may cause the stabile to collapse.

1. *A Flower Bouquet.* The younger child will enjoy making a flower bouquet and will not be especially interested in the principles involved. Ahead of time, the adult leader should dip white pipe cleaners in green tempera paint to which some white glue has been added. Be sure these are dry before the child begins to use them.

Help the children bend one end of the pipe cleaner into a circle or at least bend about ½ inch into a half circle. Then push the straight end of the pipe cleaner through a hole in a cupcake paper and arrange the bent circle flat against the inside bottom of the paper. Use white glue where the pipe cleaner goes through the hole, and then glue a gummed flower seal to the circle of pipe cleaner inside the cupcake paper. Leaves may be added to the green stem if desired.

After the flowers are made, put some plaster of Paris in a plastic margarine tub or the plastic lid from an aerosol can. When it is almost set, each flower stem or several twisted together can be pushed down into the plaster of Paris.

2. *Telling About a Country.* Children can use stabiles to tell about a country, using flags, pictures, small objects, or other symbols of a country or people. Use a piece of wood or a log for a holder. Drill a small hole in the base for each wire, insert the wire and glue in place. After the glue is dry, wires can be bent into different positions and items attached to their ends. Some objects can be hung from a bend in the wire; others can have the wire stuck through them and still others can be glued to the wire. After all items are attached, the wires may need to be bent some more to create a pleasing arrangement.

Note: Heavier items (like a small stone or a seashell) will have to be glued onto the top of the wire first and fixed into the base when dry. The base may need to be laid on its side for the glue to dry. This will help avoid the frustration of having an object keep falling off the wire while you wait for the glue to dry.

A Variation: The stabile idea can be used to create a sculpture or carving (in clay or wood) of a child holding a kite or balloon. Arrange one end of the wire in the child's hand and attach the kite or balloon at the other end. The kite or balloon can also be made of wire and covered with a piece of colored tissue or cellophane.

stenciling

WHAT IT IS—

Stenciling is the process of creating a design by covering part of a surface with a pattern and applying paint to the rest of the surface. This includes creation of the stencil; however, for younger children who are not sufficiently skilled at cutting, the stencil may be prepared beforehand. In this section we will deal with making stencils and stenciling on cloth, paper, wood and tin.

Young children can use a stencil long before they can cut out designs themselves. They enjoy placing a leaf or some other shape on a surface and painting around it with a spray bottle or toothbrush and piece of screen. This latter process, sometimes called spatter painting, is included here because it is the reverse of the process used by older children. That is, the design itself is not painted, but the area around it is; with stencils cut by older children, the center of the design is painted and the area around it is not.

WHEN AND WHERE TO USE IT—

Children can use the stenciling process when they want to create a design with some sections painted

and some sections unpainted. They can also use stencils to make multiple copies of a design.

You will need adequate space for a work area for the stencil making and painting. In order to complete the entire process, including planning the design, making the stencil, painting it, letting it dry, and pressing it for permanence, the children will need a good block of time. For those old enough to sustain interest over a longer period, the process can be divided into three stages: preparing the stencil, painting, pressing.

WHY CHILDREN USE IT—

Stenciling allows children to:
—explore shapes and outline designs like squares, circles, leaves, grasses, feathers, etc.
—create designs related to a certain topic or seasonal emphasis
—create designs in various levels of difficulty
—produce multiple copies of a desired design
—produce designs on clothing, household items, walls, toys and surfaces besides paper.

WHAT CHILDREN NEED—

—work area, including table surface, newspaper pads, push pins or thumbtacks, blotter paper or paper towels for placing under cloth, china or plastic plates for mixing paints and working stiff brush
—paper for stencil (mimeograph paper, oaktag, thin cardboard), single-edged razor or utility knife, crayon for drawing, pencil, carbon paper
—paraffin wax, tin can, baking pan
—surfaces on which to paint, including paper (colored or white), cloth, walls, tins, wood, etc.
—nature items (leaves, grasses, feathers)
—household items (spoons, forks, cups, etc.)
—shapes (circles, squares, triangles, etc.)
—paints, including tempera of all colors (see below for specific types of paint for various projects)
—white shoe polish, window screen, ruler, toothbrush
—solvent for some types of paint (turpentine, paint thinner)
—rags for clean-up
—window cleaner spray bottle or insect spray gun

HOW TO DO IT—

Simple Stenciling with Young Children

Young children will enjoy spattering paint over a shape and then lifting to see the results. Collect nature items like leaves, grasses, stones and bark. Or suggest that children use washable household items, like measuring spoons, forks, small measuring cups, plates and other everyday items.

Circles, squares, triangles and irregular shapes can be cut out by an adult or older children. Have the younger children arrange the shapes on a piece of paper placed on a pad of newspapers. You may want to hold light objects in place with a push pin or straight pin. Show children how to spray from above and cover all the spaces around the outlines. If paint brushes are used, help children learn how to paint carefully first around the edges of the stencils and then fill in all other exposed spaces. (See instructions following.) When the paintings have started to dry, carefully pick up the shapes to reveal the stenciled painting.

Suggestions for Spraying. Use tempera paints in a plastic window cleaner spray bottle or insect spray gun. Young children will need some practice. Older children can use aerosol spray cans, especially if they are painting on wood, such as toy boxes or outdoor play equipment.

Spatter Technique. Dip a toothbrush in tempera paint or white shoe polish and rub the bristles across the edge of a ruler or over a small piece of window screen.

Making Stencils

Children can either draw their own designs or find them on wallpaper, cloth, in magazines or in other places. Begin with a simple design with only a few open spaces. On heavy absorbent paper—mimeograph paper is good—copy the design in the size desired. Now study it carefully. Are there any very large areas? These can be made into smaller areas by leaving narrow (⅛-inch) sections of paper between smaller open spaces. For example, flower petals, leaves and stems can be separated by a ⅛-inch strip. If you draw around each open space with a crayon and cut out the open spaces, the width of the crayon lines will be sufficient to hold the pieces together.

The above suggestions are for a fairly simple design that can be cut out of one stencil and painted in one color, in one operation. (See illustration, p. 52, for a simple Pennsylvania Dutch design.)

Older children can do much more intricate stenciling, making two or more stencils and painting with different colors in several steps. The various stencils each have different combinations of holes cut out and the child paints all of the openings in one stencil, lets that dry, and then paints all the openings of another.

With multiple stencils, the design must be placed in exactly the same position on each stencil. It is usually best to use carbon paper so you can draw the design on all the stencils in one operation. All sections to be painted the same color should be numbered with the same number (or shaded in with pencil) before cutting. With careful drawing and careful cutting, the adjoining sections will be perfectly lined up. The illustration shows a rose pattern that requires four different stencils.

After the design is drawn, each stencil should be coated with wax to strengthen it before the individual sections are cut out. Melt a bar of paraffin wax in a tin can placed over boiling water. (Note: Do not heat paraffin directly over a flame, as it can catch fire.) Pour melted wax into a baking pan, dip the stencil sheet into the wax and hold it up to dry. When dry and stiff, cut out all the parts numbered with the same number. Children should use a utility knife or a single-edged razor blade. Check to see that all have been properly cut by placing all the stencils directly over one another. Hold up to a bright light and see if any section does not appear to have been cut out at all. Each area should be cut out in only one stencil.

Using the Stencil and Paint

Stenciling can be done on paper, matchstick blinds, cloth, wood, tin trays and cans, boxes, etc. First,

make sure the surface is clean and free of oil. Some surfaces may need one coat of paint as a background before stenciling. Cloth should be washed and ironed to remove any filler or starch.

The following types of paint may be used:
—Enamels—floors, wood trays and boxes, tin
—Enamel or nongloss wall paint—walls
—Textile paint—cloth (mix as directed on the jars).

Stencils can be cleaned with a soft cloth soaked in turpentine and then reused.

Whatever its nature, the surface should be as level as possible during painting so that the paint will not run. Place the surface on a pad of newspapers. If you are stenciling on cloth, place a blotter or paper toweling directly under the cloth to soak up any paint that penetrates. Lay the stencil in place and pin if necessary. Paint the largest areas first, using a stiff brush that has a flat end. Always slide the brush off the stencil toward the surface being painted. This makes for a sharper edge and gives better control of the stenciling than does painting parallel to the stencil edge.

When using multiple stencils, be sure to let the paint dry between each step. A second color can be placed on adjoining sections best when the first color is dry. After the last stencil has been painted, allow the entire project to dry at least 24 hours, especially with stencils done on cloth. When dry, you can cover the cloth with brown paper and iron it to set the colors permanently. With stencils done on wood or tin you may want to cover the entire design with a coat of clear varnish after the drying period.

stitchery

WHAT IT IS—

By stitchery we mean the process of applying designs and objects to cloth with threads or yarn. The emphasis here is on creative use of materials to produce an attractive and pleasing design (for utilitarian aspects, see Sewing).

After trying mesh weaving (see Weaving) or making string designs using glue (see String), boys and girls may want to experiment with sewing yarn designs on cloth. Stitchery is the next logical step. Several stitches can be learned easily so that the child's early exploring with needle, thread, and cloth will be fun. After stitchery, the next logical step is sewing (see Sewing), which is often more product-oriented and has more rules. Stitchery is fun and should be approached that way.

WHEN AND WHERE TO DO IT—

Children can experiment with stitchery when they wish to use needle, thread or yarn, and material. They can do it on their own or as part of a group project.

Stitchery can be done wherever there is space to sit down. A table is handy for materials, but another chair or the floor works equally well. Few tools are necessary, and needle, thread and fabric can be taken anywhere. Make sure good lighting is available.

WHY CHILDREN DO IT—

Stitchery allows children to:
—explore freely the use of fabric and threads
—learn beginning sewing skills with freedom
—realize how these beginning techniques can be used later in making useful items such as clothing and household articles
—design stitchery pieces in appealing shapes and colors.

WHAT CHILDREN NEED—

—ruler, scissors, pins
—sewing needles with large eyes (tapestry needles for young children; sharp needles for older children or for tightly woven fabrics)
—fabrics (loose weaves like burlap, linen, hopsacking; tight weaves for contrasts; large pieces for some items and scraps for other purposes; be sure to have many colors and patterns available)

—threads (various colors of thread and yarns, including metallic threads; a heavy button or rug thread—#8— will show up well in a design)

—decorative materials (beads, buttons, suede pieces, artificial fur pieces, fringe, edgings, sequins, etc.)

HOW TO DO IT—

Many simple stitchery projects can give children experience with using needles, threads or yarns, and fabric. Decorative designs that can be hung or displayed for their own beauty, banners that provide a visual message, place mats, covers for books and notebooks, pictures sewn on cloth—these are a few examples. See Sewing and Dolls (Volume 1) for suggestions about sewing clothing in either life size or miniature size.

Children will want to learn a few simple stitches as they gain experience. The accompanying illustrations show some of the easiest ones.

Some stitchery patterns give a feeling of motion, while others provide depth. Some outline a shape; others detail parts of a shape or tie together many shapes. To make letters or words, running or couching stitches are appropriate. Large spaces can be filled in with cross stitch, French knots, bundles, or daisies. Encourage the children to experiment with many different kinds of stitches to find the most pleasing patterns and designs.

Here are some beginning projects:

1. *A First Piece: A Sampler.* Children can use whatever yarns and fabrics are available to make a sampler that shows a particular stitch (or several stitches). This is a good way to try out new stitches. Let the children create their own designs or arrange the stitching in whatever way they want.

Some leaders like to make up a sample piece of fabric for each stitch. Or you can make a simple enlarged drawing of the stitch for children to refer to.

2. *Banners.* Banners can be made with many combinations of fabrics and stitches. See Banners (Volume 1) for details.

3. *Fabric Collage.* Apply the collage technique (see Volume 1) by using a variety of colors and textures,

BASIC STITCHES

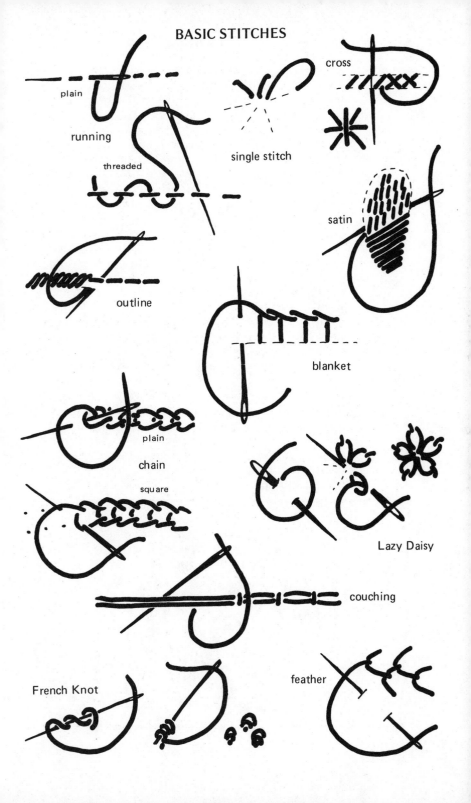

highlighting or outlining certain parts of the collage with stitchery. For example, you can use the couching stitch with a smaller thread of contrasting color to go around a thicker piece of yarn. Fabric collages can be an arrangement of materials and stitches that represents an object, person, scene, etc; or they can be merely a pleasing mixture of colors and textures. An example of the former would be a collage of the three Wise Men, done in richly-colored velvet with metallic brocades and fringes as decorations.

4. *Stitchery Trims.* Stitchery can be used to decorate many common objects—for example, jeans, shirts, napkins, place mats, pillow covers, towels, etc.

5. *A Thread Picture.* Children can create a stitchery picture by drawing a scene or design on a plain fabric (muslin or linen) background. Then they sew in the picture using stitches of various kinds and many color combinations. Help them plan the picture or scene carefully by suggesting that they keep in mind as they sketch it on the fabric how they will stitch it in later. Beginners should keep the picture simple!

6. *Applique.* This technique involves sewing one piece of fabric onto another so that the first piece appears to be a part of the original, or looks "painted on." This involves sewing completely around the appliqued pieces so that none of its cut edges show. Obviously, children can combine applique with many other techniques.

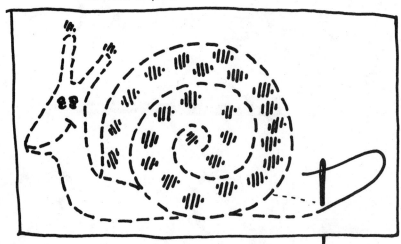

An interesting variation is the cut-away applique technique, where several layers of fabric are superimposed on one another and appliqued onto a background piece. Then areas are cut away from one, two or more layers, exposing the various layers underneath. Each cut-away area is then appliqued, creating unique combinations and patterns. This art form has been perfected by the San Blas Islanders. (For details see page 63 in *Making Things* by Ann Wiseman, listed in the Bibliography.)

storytelling

WHAT IT IS—

Storytelling is the process of sharing a story aloud with one or more persons. It can be done with varying degrees of success by children of all ages, as well as by adult leaders. See also related sections:

Books and Stories, Drama, Flannel Board, all in Volume 1; Movement (including Pantomime), Pictures, Play Writing, Puppets, in Volume 2; Story Writing.

WHEN TO DO IT—

Use storytelling when a particular story can best be studied or enjoyed through sharing with one or more children, or when a particular story has been found that can help achieve certain purposes of the children or leader through telling in a group.

Stories can be created to achieve such purposes as helping children understand a certain person better; helping children get a better picture or imagine what a certain time period or event was like; or helping children have fun imagining stories.

WHERE TO DO IT—

Storytelling can be done wherever a storyteller and listeners can gather for sharing. Some stories may require certain settings for a mood or background, but it is usually best to let the storyteller create these without the aid of a lot of physical props.

WHY CHILDREN DO IT—

Storytelling is important for children:
—to develop vocabulary, ability to communicate and to listen, as well as to visualize
—to increase comprehension skills, imagination and creativity
—to understand and enjoy books and stories one might not be able to read alone
—to share in a warm, personal experience with others
—to personalize the sharing of stories and information
—to adapt a story for the particular needs of an audience
—to find the best versions of stories to use again and again.

WHAT CHILDREN NEED—

—stories suitable for telling
—interested listeners
—leaders who are patient and accepting as they help children learn to tell stories, and who are spontaneous and sensitive when they themselves tell stories
—a friendly, accepting atmosphere

HOW TO DO IT—

Children as Storytellers

If children are going to be the storytellers, they should be given lots of freedom to share stories in ways most natural for them. Do not expect children to be little adults when they tell stories; they cannot do an adult job of storytelling.

Help children to think about how the story can be made most interesting and fun for those hearing it. Once a few simple guidelines are clear, they should be freed to prepare their stories with as little adult intervention as possible.

Here are some guidelines in the form of questions for children to think about as they get ready to tell a story.

1. *The people (or animals)*

Who are the most interesting people (characters)? Which ones shall we include?

How can we describe them so our listeners will see them in their own minds? What can we tell about their faces? Their clothing? Their size? Their personality or the type of person they are? The way they talk? Act? Treat others?

2. *The places*

How can we describe the places in the story so that our listeners will get a picture in their minds? Should we describe houses? Towns? Roads?

Is the story in the present day? Or do we have to tell what it was like in another time in history?

3. *The actions (what happens)*

How can we start the story with something exciting that is happening and that will immediately get the attention of our listeners?

What events should follow? In what order? How shall we describe them?

What is the most important part (climax) of the story? Do we get to that part fast enough? Too fast? Too slowly? How can we make it exciting?

How do we end the story? Do we end quickly enough, but not too quickly? Will our listeners feel satisfied when they have heard the story?

4. *How to tell it*

Shall just one person tell it? Shall we act it out while one person tells it? Should we use puppets while someone tells it? Would pictures help?

How can we prepare our listeners for our story?

As children focus their thinking and planning, they will be able to make suggestions of their own and choose from among the best suggestions as they actually prepare their stories.

One good rule to follow in helping children tell stories is, *Keep it short!* During the planning process, children should discover if their story is going to be too long for their audience. If older children are planning to tell a story to a group of four- or five-year-olds, for example, they will need to plan for a much shorter story than if they are preparing something for their own age group.

Adults as Storytellers

The same guiding questions apply when adult leaders prepare to tell a story to children. Here are some additional suggestions for adults:

1. Choose stories carefully, picking those that fit your purpose and your group, and that you enjoy yourself.

2. Practice enough that you can believe the story you tell.

3. Be dynamic; put yourself into the telling.

4. Get physically close to your audience. Although you may feel awkward with your adult body on the floor along with the children, they will respond to your closeness.

5. Prepare your audience. Create a setting and a mood before you begin. Let them know the time, place, characters, and their relationships. Use some action to set the mood—light a flashlight for a nighttime mystery; put on a hat that fits one of the characters.

6. Get the story moving quickly. Decide ahead of time on some clearly defined beginning incidents that involve a major character.

7. Keep the story moving through a series of well-ordered events. Learn the story incident-by-incident rather than word-by-word. See your story whole in terms of this series of related incidents. When the story hangs together in this way it begins to live for you, and you will be able to make it live for others. When you know the sequence of events, put them in words that are appropriate for each audience.

8. End the story in a satisfying way. Plan carefully the transition from climax to conclusion; don't make the conclusion too long in coming. When the story is finished, let it speak for itself. Do not moralize or point out a lesson.

9. Stay with your story line, but keep the attention span of your listeners in mind. Make adjustments as you go, keeping the basic story intact but altering the details as necessary for your particular audience.

10. Keep clear the distinction between story-reading and storytelling. In storytelling you have the story clearly in mind and you tell it, without depending on

a book that is likely to get between you and your listeners.

11. Practice every story before you tell it. Try using a mirror or tape recorder. Make the story special for every audience, no matter how many times you have told it before!

12. Provide time for children to reflect on and talk about the story. Let them say what the story means for them.

13. Remember that young children like repetition, so use lots of it. Stories should have a single theme and few characters. Since many young children will profit more from an experience that is both oral and visual, plan to use pictures and objects with young children.

14. Older children will enjoy open-ended stories that allow them to participate by completing a story that has been told up to a certain point.

Choosing Story Material

Among the many sources are church curriculum materials, which usually have stories in student books and story papers that lend themselves to telling. Be sure to adapt and prepare each story as suggested above. Your choice of material should always be guided by your purposes.

Stories for pure enjoyment will be available in your public library and in many good collections of children's stories. (See also the Bibliography at the end of this volume.)

string

WHAT IT IS—

String, for our purposes, is cord, thread or yarn and may be used for many different creative purposes. Before they learn stitching, children can explore many other things to do with string. They can use it as a toy spinner; put it through holes in wood to make a picture or design; do mesh weaving with yarn; glue string to paper, wood or cloth; or some other creative activity.

WHEN AND WHERE TO USE IT—

Children can experiment with string at any time and in almost any place. They will be limited only by the need for the right kind of materials and some ideas for what to do with them.

WHY CHILDREN USE IT—

String allows children to:
—learn to manipulate various size pieces
—make many designs
—experiment with the many available colors and textures
—discover the possibilities in three-dimensional creations.

WHAT CHILDREN NEED—

—a wide assortment of strings, yarns, threads and cords; shoelaces in various sizes and colors
—scissors
—white glue
—wooden frame, pegboard squares, asbestos tiles, boxes
—golf tees
—construction paper
—hole puncher

HOW TO USE IT—

Most of the fun in using string comes from letting the design evolve as the child glues down the threads or winds them into various shapes and patterns.

Note: Create a simple lacing end by wrapping a small piece of masking tape around one end of a piece of yarn or cord, or by coating the end with white glue to keep it from fraying and to stiffen it for going through holes.

1. *String Lacing Cards.* This project will be best for younger children. Cut out an interesting picture and glue it onto a piece of light cardboard. When the glue

is dry, punch holes every half inch or so around the edges of the design or figure. Shoelaces or brightly colored yarn with one end taped can be used for lacing in and out among the holes. *Note:* Be sure to tie a knot in the opposite end, so that young children are not frustrated by pulling their string or yarn all the way out of the lacing card.

2. *String Boards.* Cut a piece of pegboard into a 12-inch square or a rectangle 12 x 18 inches, or use a square acoustical ceiling tile. Arrange a number of golf tees in a design on the board. Provide lots of colorful pieces of string and let the children make designs by winding the string between the tees, going from one to another, coming around and back, creating many interesting patterns. Suggest that the children look at their designs. Ask questions like, "What does it remind you of? What might you change if you did it again?"

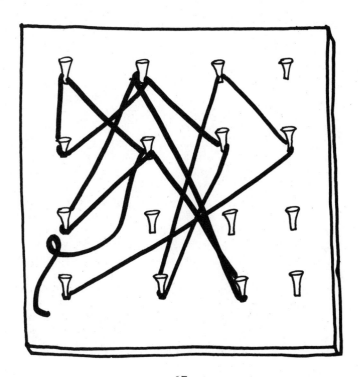

3. *Glued String Designs.* Children can create a design on construction paper by gluing down pieces of string. They can either arrange the string and then glue it down, or they can release a thin line of white glue onto the construction paper and then lay the string or yarn along the glue line. After this is dry, the children may decide to fill in other areas by gluing string down to fill up the space with solid color and texture. Other areas may be left plain. Let the children create their own designs and decorate them as they wish.

4. *String Up a Box.* Using a cardboard box (shoebox size or smaller), punch holes around the outside edges and at the back. Adults will need to help children with the holes that are not near the edges, where a hole punch can be used; try using a sharp pointed pair of scissors, the prong of a cooking fork, the point of a skewer or some other sharp pointed instrument, but be careful! Now encourage the children to string a three-dimensional design in and out of the holes, front to back, side to side, top to bottom. Some may want to paint the inside of their boxes first.

5. *String a Flat Design.* Use a cardboard loom for a base (see instructions in Weaving) but make cuts on all four sides instead of on just two. Children can then create interesting designs by wrapping the string or yarn from one cut to another, making angles, going up, down, and around, as well as over other colors. Encourage the children to see how many different designs they can create. Ends of the yarn can be glued on the back.

6. *Geometric String Designs.* Draw a simple geometric shape like an oval, circle, diamond, etc. on an index card (5 x 8-inch) or light poster board. The shape should be at least 4 inches wide at the smallest part. Mark off dots about 1/4 inch apart all the way around the outside of the cardboard, and push a needle through each. Divide the entire design into four equal parts and number each part on the back: 1, 2, 3, 4. Then thread a sharp sewing needle with one or two colors of sewing thread, knot it near the end, and bring it through (from the back) any hole in

the #1 section. Then go across the front of the design to a hole in the #2 section, going through to the back and out to the front of an adjacent hole. Then move on to the #3 and #4 sections. The child continues in any pattern that is pleasing. A particular hole can be used more than once. Encourage the children to explore with different designs. When finished, glue thread ends onto the back.

For variations try a different sequence of sewing, such as using every other hole. Or change the colors of the thread. Or try another shape of index card or poster board.

These geometric designs look nice when framed. For an older child who wants to go further, suggest making a design over a larger piece of cardboard covered with velvet or no-wale corduroy.

WHERE TO GET MORE HELP—

Ellison, Elsie C., *Fun With Lines and Curves*. New York: Lothrop, Lee and Shepard Company, 1972. 95 pp. $4.95.

Symbols

WHAT THEY ARE—

A symbol is a shape, sign or design that stands for some idea or that has a special meaning for certain persons.

People have made symbols all through history, from early pictures on cave walls to symbols children make today when they use a group of chairs to represent an airplane.

Older elementary children can be intentional in their study of symbols.

WHEN TO USE THEM—

Children can learn to use and enjoy symbols when they are studying how persons have captured an idea or concept in visual form, including ways Christians have experienced and expressed their faith. As a basis, children can discover how persons have always used symbols to express ideas. Study of symbols is most appropriate with older children who can conceptualize the idea represented by a sign or picture.

WHERE TO USE OR MAKE THEM—

Since we are surrounded by symbols every day, children can study them in many places. Many ideas suggested here will involve boys and girls in searching out symbols in various places. To reproduce symbols or create symbols of their own, children will need a place where they can use the necessary materials for whatever process they are using.

WHY CHILDREN USE OR MAKE THEM—

Symbols allow children to:
—communicate their feelings or thoughts

—experience the creation of a new symbolic way of expressing something
—express graphically ideas, thoughts or realities that they cannot duplicate verbally
—discover how persons before them have communicated certain ideas or concepts in graphic forms
—participate in the Christian faith as they understand the symbols used to express religious beliefs.

WHAT CHILDREN NEED—

—a growing alertness, coming from study and observation, to those symbols that are used around them
—good source books on symbols (several are listed in the Bibliography)
—opportunities to express their own thoughts and ideas in symbols
—necessary materials and supplies to make symbols (see specific suggestions below)

HOW TO USE OR MAKE THEM—

Common symbols all around us include those that stand for the brands of gasoline or food or clothing we buy. Symbols can be experienced through actions such as a wave or a frown or a kiss.

Discuss these with children when appropriate. At another time trace the use of symbols in the history of the church. Begin to make a study of the symbols around you—in the community, in the church building. Discover what you can about the symbols of other cultures.

Activities to Help Children Learn About Symbols

The following activities are designed to help boys and girls be more conscious of symbols:

1. *An "I Spy" Game.* Play a game: "I spy a round symbol of a dove. Who can tell me where it is? Do you know what it means?" "I spy a symbol for the birth of Jesus. What does the symbol show? Who knows what it is called?"

2. *A Symbol Scavenger Hunt.* Give out lists of symbols to be found in the area (in the community, in a building, along a street) and see who can find the largest number. This can be done in teams of two,

with each team writing down exactly where they find the symbol and what it looks like.

3. *A Symbol Walk.* What are some symbols of companies and organizations around you? This activity takes you into symbols of advertising and brand names as a way to remember a product. Have the children make a list of those they can think of. Then take a walk and add to the list all those you see. When you come back, children can make a collage or display of various trademarks and symbols.

4. *Study Christian Symbols.* Deal with Christian symbols as we know them today. What was the earliest symbol? (The fish) How was it used? (Early Christians identified each other when one started drawing the fish symbol and the other completed it.) How many types of crosses are there? Children can look them up, draw them and perhaps make a display. What are some other Christian symbols? (Get a good source book on symbols and make a special study of those used in your church building or community.) One child could be responsible for finding out about each symbol and could then make up a Fact Card to be used by everyone.

Older children might create a set of Christian symbols for the congregation out of papier mâché (see Papier Mâché, Volume 2). These can be painted and used for decoration and study in various rooms in the church building.

5. *Numbers and Colors.* Do some research on numbers with symbolic meaning and the colors in the Christian liturgical year.

6. *Flags.* Study flags of countries, as well as school flags and religious flags and banners, as symbols.

Ways to Use Symbols

The following are activities involving symbols:

1. *A Symbol Notebook.* In this variation of the fact card idea in #4, children gather together on notebook sheets information about the symbols they have found. At the top of the page would be a drawing of the symbol; at the bottom a brief explanation of its meaning and location in the church building or community.

2. *Symbols of Persons.* Children can make a study of the symbols of leaders in church history or create their own symbols for those persons. An example would be symbols for the disciples.

3. *Symbols of the Season.* Suggest that children explore the seasons of the church year and create their own symbols for them (Advent, Christmastide, Epiphany, etc.). They could also create symbols for the seasons of the calendar year (spring, summer, fall, winter).

4. *Symbols on Banners.* Create some new symbols for a season (like Easter) or for your local congregation or your own group. Then display these symbols on banners (see Banners, Volume 1).

5. *Making Symbols Visible.* Explore with children different techniques for making copies of symbols. They could use potato printing, block printing, tissue paper transparencies, creative stitchery, and many others. (See many other sections for techniques.)

6. *Write a Symbol Guide.* Older elementary children can plan and write a tour guide to locally-used symbols and their meaning. Have this mimeographed and let the children lead some adults on the tour, telling the meaning of the various symbols.

7. *Chrismon Tree.* Make a Chrismon tree for Christmas. This is a green tree decorated only with symbols for Jesus, including many different crosses, fish, Chi Rho and stars. Use white Styrofoam for the symbols and decorate with silver and gold glitter, metallic braid and pearl beads. These are lovely on a dark green tree.

tapes

WHAT THEY ARE—

Audio recordings made on tape recorders and preserved on magnetic tape are usually of two kinds: (1)

those made on ¼-inch magnetic tape on an open reel for use in a reel-to-reel tape recorder and (2) those made on ⅛-inch magnetic tape in a plastic cassette for use in audio cassette tape recorders. The audio cassette has increased tremendously in popularity because of its simplicity and easy portability. Reel-to-reel tape recording has the advantage of high quality sound reproduction.

WHEN TO USE THEM—

Children can use tapes in a formal classroom setting or informally on their own. When children need to preserve some kind of sound input, the tape recorder will be their most effective tool. There are also times when a particular prerecorded tape can help achieve a purpose.

WHERE TO USE THEM—

The cassette tape recorder is portable and children can use a battery-powered one almost anywhere. Reel-to-reel tape recorders normally must be plugged into an electric power source.

There is almost no limit on the type of audio input children might use in making their own tape recordings. They may interview particular persons or record certain sounds in many places. Children can listen to tapes almost anywhere. They may listen privately in one corner of a classroom with a headset or earplug. Or children can use tapes in a total group, such as when a taped hymn or song is part of a worship service.

WHY CHILDREN USE THEM—

Tapes allow children to:
—make their own recordings of almost any sound input, including music, the spoken voice and sounds typical of a certain place
—preserve for future use sounds that may not be available later
—create their own audio background, either with music or from some other sound source
—listen, either privately or in groups, to learning material already prepared

74

—record their own progress in learning something, such as singing a new song or telling a story
—have fun experimenting with sound and the recording of sound, particularly their own voices.

WHAT CHILDREN NEED—

—a tape recorder (either cassette or reel-to-reel)
—blank tape (with reel-to-reel children will need a reel of tape and an empty take-up reel; with cassette children will need blank cassettes, preferably C-30s, with 15 minutes per side for a total of 30 minutes, or C-60s, with 30 minutes per side for a total of 60 minutes)
—instructions on how to use the tape recorder
—lots of good ideas on what to record

HOW TO USE THEM—

Getting Ready to Record

Choose a place with a minimum of such outside noise as traffic or persons talking. Arrange the tape recorder and microphone ahead of time, according to the kind of sound input you will have. To record a group of people talking, place the microphone in the center of the area from which the voices will come. If you place the microphone on a table and it does not have its own stand, arrange it on a folded handkerchief or some other sound-absorbing material.

Be sure the persons who are going to speak into the microphone are familiar with their materials; if they are to read it word for word, see that they have practiced to achieve a natural rhythm. Be sure persons are seated in proper relationship to the microphone and to one another, and ask that they keep to a minimum the shuffling of papers.

The operator should check out all equipment ahead of time. This will avoid the frustration of finding that you have been missing what should have been recorded. On many tape recorders the operator can use an earphone to check what is being picked up.

Making the Recording

Have the recorder set with controls properly arranged in the "Record" position. Some microphones have a remote control button so that all other controls can be preset and the microphone button moved to the "On" position when you are ready to begin. (See "Some Useful Hints" for a suggestion about timing the beginning of the recording.)

If you are reusing tape, the tape recorder will automatically erase previously recorded material. You may want to record a few moments of silence after the actual recording is completed to prevent previously recorded material from following immediately after the newly recorded material.

Playing It Back

To listen to your recording, rewind the tape and play it again. You can redo certain spots, if necessary. Listen carefully to the section you want to redo, counting as you listen to establish how many counts will cover the space of time. Then rewind to the beginning of the place you want to redo, put the microphone in the "Record" position and (without making any sounds) count out the proper number of counts. Then stop the recorder. Now listen to it again and decide if you have erased the part you wanted to. Then either leave it blank or record a new section.

Ways Children Can Use Tape Recorders

While many of the following suggestions can be done with either cassette or reel-to-reel recorders, others will work best with the easily portable cassette recorders, which many children now have available at home. Although each idea is independent, many are interrelated, but they are listed in no particular order of priority.

1. Songs can be recorded on cassettes, using piano, Autoharp, guitar or recordings provided with curriculum materials. Such tapes are extremely useful in helping groups learn songs, since they can be repeated as children learn the music and words. Taped songs can also be used in worship services. Each song should be recorded on a separate side of a cassette, and they should be clearly labeled for future reference.

2. Children can record sounds to share later with

others—sounds of the street, sounds of the playground, sounds of a farm or a zoo or some other place they have visited. Such a tape will help to heighten the children's awareness of the sounds that are all around them. (See also "Listen to the World Around You" in Sensory Experiences.)

3. Younger children who do not yet write with ease can record conversations, story ideas, suggestions for play scenarios, ideas for how to carry something out. The teacher may then write these suggestions on newsprint or tablet paper for group use.

4. Children's conversations can be recorded. Such recordings will often increase the child's confidence that he or she has something to say or ideas that are worthwhile. Sometimes these conversations are best not shared with others; at other times sharing is permissible.

5. Small committees of older elementaries can tape reports to share with their total group. Such tapes might include information they want to share or conversations or interviews with certain persons.

6. Materials from student books or other reading books can be recorded for individual use. Good readers among older children can make such recordings so that younger children or those who did not yet read the material can follow along in their books, using the pictures and other activities that accompany the story.

7. To help a child who is blind or who has a reading problem, another child or an adult could tape printed material. Then the child who cannot read the words off a printed page can listen to them.

8. Record on cassette the story in a younger child's storybook. Very often these books have only small amounts of text. An audible tone, such as a click or a bell, could be used to signal time to turn the page. Then the child can look at the pictures and listen to the story at the same time.

9. Tape recorders can be used to provide instructions for a game, a puzzle, or some other learning activity. The recording can be done by a teacher or by one of the children, and then other children get their instructions from the tape.

10. The script for a puppet play can be taped ahead of time when it is still fresh and spontaneous, so children can concentrate on handling puppets.

11. Children can use the tape recorder to keep a record of their committee work, thus eliminating the need for someone to take minutes.

12. Children can exchange tapes with many other persons—for example, a child who is in the hospital or ill at home. The tape could share what the group has been doing or what they are thinking about, and could include comments or greetings or conversations directed to the sick child.

13. Exchange taped conversations with children in other places, particularly in other parts of the world. Such tapes could include songs, stories and conversation typical of the place where the child lives, providing a real cultural exchange.

14. Children can record a script or some ideas to go along with a set of slides or mounted pictures. The recording is best made when the children are putting their ideas together, so they will be spontaneous and natural. Then the recording can be used any number of times. The tape could also suggest activities for use with the slides or pictures.

15. Tapes can be used to preserve what children are doing at the beginning of a unit or at the beginning of the year. Then these tapes can be replayed at the end of a series of lessons or at the end of the year, and the children can add their current ideas. This will help them realize how they have changed and grown, and will provide a kind of historical record of the class group.

16. A filmslip or filmstrip script can be recorded on cassette so that younger children who can operate a filmstrip projector themselves can view the filmstrip and use the tape player for the audio portion.

17. Especially with younger age groups, let the children experiment simply with recording their own voices. This helps the child learn more about who he or she is, since often children are quite surprised to learn how their voices sound when recorded. Perhaps teachers can talk with young children in taped conversations for this purpose.

18. Record a group of children singing. This will help them learn a particular song and will also help them see how they sound as a singing group.

19. Record a choral reading done by a group of children.

20. Tapes can be used for review at the end of a series of sessions or sequence of activities. Use stories, songs, choral readings, reports or other things children can put on tape.

21. Children could use tapes to gather an oral history of their local congregation. Interviews with older members of the congregation who can share their recollections about early events would be useful, as would conversations with early surviving pastors. Such tapes would be a useful addition to any written records that might exist. A tape might even be preserved in a cornerstone of a church building.

22. The tape recorder can be used to help children *hear* Bible passages. Tapes could be made over a long period of time, labeled and stored for repeated use. Readers could be children, teachers, your pastor.

23. Have children put Bible passages into their own words and record these on tape. If the Bible were being written today, it might be put on tape rather than being passed orally from generation to generation before being written down.

24. During Bible study, children could do taped interviews with biblical characters as a way of getting at how those persons thought and felt during certain experiences. Children would have to do some research and study into the person's life in order to be able to respond to the interviewer's questions.

25. Tape "news reports" of certain Bible events or experiences—for example, an eyewitness account of the baptism of Jesus, Jesus' visit to the temple as a boy, the Crucifixion, or the conversion of Paul. The person making the tape would prepare a news report as if he or she had been a reporter at the event and were now reporting it to a TV or radio audience.

26. All recorded items in regular ongoing curriculum materials can be converted to cassette tape. This can include songs, dramas, open-ended stories, filmslip soundtracks, etc.

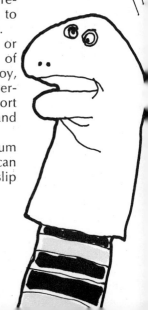

Some Useful Hints

1. If a cassette tape sticks, the tape may be wound unevenly on one of its reels and sticking against the inside of the plastic cartridge. Hold the cassette by one corner and hit it against a table top or other flat surface with a sharp blow. Be sure to hit the cassette with its flat side, so that the tape will be knocked into line with the rest of the reel again.

2. Store cassettes in their original plastic containers or in special storage cases purchased for that purpose. Be sure to label each cassette so that you know what is on each side. Pressure-sensitive labels can be obtained to fit the available space on the cassette surface. Label both the tape and the storage box and you will have the beginnings of a tape library for your group's use.

3. Choose the size of cassette according to how much you want to record on each side. Since it is difficult to find something that begins in the middle of a side, it is best to start each recording at the beginning of a side and label it as such.

4. Consult your audiovisual dealer about the best tape for recording music, especially when using cassettes. Reel-to-reel recorders work best for music, but with good tape most cassette recorders will provide satisfactory quality for classroom use.

5. There is a blank "leader" at each end of the cassette tape that does not record. If the tape is stopped at the very beginning of the reel, about five seconds are needed for this leader to pass the recording head. If you begin speaking or playing into the microphone before this time elapses, the first part of your recording will be lost. If children remember to say slowly and silently to themselves, "One thousand, two thousand, three thousand, four thousand, five thousand," they can then safely begin the recording.

6. To prevent a tape from being erased, knock out the little squares of plastic at the back corners of the cassette cartridge (see illus.) when it is in position in the machine. When these square holes are open, the tape cannot be rerecorded. If you later decide to rerecord, cover up those holes with a small piece of masking tape.

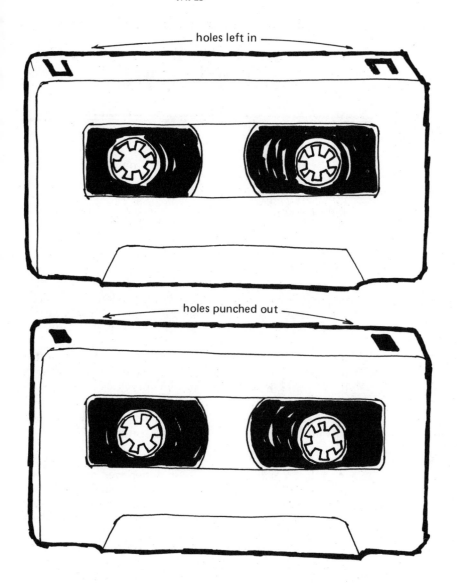

holes left in

holes punched out

7. See Records for suggestions on using tapes with individuals or small groups, including instructions for a homemade listening center that allows as many as six persons to listen at the same time.

television

WHAT IT IS—

We refer here to prepared programs broadcast through a television set, and exclude from this discussion any kind of impromptu recording of picture and/or sound. (See Film, Volume 1, or Videotape for impromptu recording.)

Included here are black and white and color broadcasts, through both commercial and public television stations. Two additional sources for television broadcasting promise to become more important in the future. One is cable television, a system by which subscribers' regular sets can be connected to a vastly expanded system of television broadcast channels. The implications for church education have yet to be fully explored. The second source is the cassette format, by which a television receiver can (1) play back through its own system previously recorded television tape housed in a cassette or (2) both record and play back material received from regular broadcast sources.

WHEN TO USE IT—

Children can use television whenever appropriate program material is being broadcast. Usually TV programs are broadcast at times when classroom viewing is impossible. Thus there is often a delay between viewing and any discussion in a class or group. Cable TV offers the potential of many more selections being available at any one time; thus television may eventually be more widely used in the classroom. With cassette TV, programs can be recorded and played back later at any convenient time.

WHERE TO USE IT—

Children will probably view many television programs in the home, and only a few in the church education setting. With the potential of cable TV and cassette TV, television use within the classroom context may increase considerably in the future.

WHY CHILDREN USE IT—

Television allows children to:
—view appropriate prepared material in a familiar medium
—gain certain information and/or experiences that they could not get firsthand
—share a common experience in viewing or talking about programs with other children, family and friends
—experience, in picture and sound, stories from literature and real events from faraway places
—entertain themselves by forgetting their immediate situation and living out a story or play.

WHAT CHILDREN NEED—

—television set
—any necessary preparation if a group is going to talk about the program later, i.e., specific persons to watch for, questions to keep in mind, etc.
—listings of projected programing on the local stations
—listeners' guides that are often available for specific programs from stations, networks or sponsors

HOW TO USE IT—

Helping Children with Their Television Viewing

How would you answer a fifth grader's question, "How can I tell if a television program is going to be good?" This is a mature question for a ten-year-old, and one many adults need to deal with in their own television viewing.

Perhaps adults should help children become more adept at evaluating what they are viewing, rather than criticizing them for spending so many hours watching poor quality programs.

Suggest the following guidelines to children for thinking about a television program.

1. Comedy: Is it fun to watch? What does the program say about human beings? Are the comic incidents believable? Or just pure fun? What skills are needed by the actors?

2. Sports programs: Are the players following good sportsmanship rules? Does the program demonstrate real athletic skill or is it commercial demonstration?

3. Drama: Do the characters seem lifelike and believable? Is the story true to life as you know it? True to another historical period? How do the persons in the program treat one another? Would you want the main character for a friend or neighbor?

4. Commercials: Do they help you feel good about yourself? Are they giving you information you need to make up your own mind?

Planning a Session Around a Television Program

Here are some suggestions for using a particular television program as part of your group's learning experience.

1. *Background.* Make available some background information on the program, especially if it is a drama, classic story, etc. What information would be helpful for the children to have prior to the viewing? You may have to do some research, read newspaper publicity, or write or call the television station for information.

2. *Viewing.* If possible, arrange for the group to view the program in their own homes or in small groups, rather than in one large group. In large groups, some children will have difficulty seeing the screen unless a large set is available. Give each person special things to look for or a specific character to follow throughout the program. Place these names or questions on cards and have each person draw one.

3. *Sharing.* a. Group Discussion. If the sharing is to take place right after the viewing, take a few moments for a break and then begin. Use questions like these: What was the main event? Who were the important characters? What was the main action? What was the message of the show, in one sentence? What do you think of the solutions found for the problems faced by the characters? What was the turning point in the action?

With a lighter type of program, you may ask questions about personal preference rather than in-depth questions.

b. Panel Discussion. If the discussion takes place some time after the viewing, you might prefer to have a panel react to the program. At the time of viewing, several questions might be asked and discussed by small viewing groups. Later, with the entire group, a panel representative from each small group would share in further discussion and thinking.

4. *Going Beyond the Story.* After discussing the program itself, the group might engage in some "What if . . ." discussion: What if one character had been changed? What if one particular event had been changed? What solutions would you have suggested to the characters if those changes had taken place?

This allows the children to partially reconstruct the story, so that they begin to see some other possibilities and evaluate for themselves the way the story was carried out.

Adapting Quiz Shows

Quiz and game shows often can be adapted for the classroom. For a good review activity, children can integrate some of the material they have been studying into the format of a favorite television quiz or game show. Let the children themselves do as much of the adapting as possible.

Cable Television

Cable television is now a reality in many communities, but generally speaking, church educators have not explored its possibilities. Since each community system operates on a localized basis under different regulations, teachers and leaders in each community need to investigate their own system and discover the potentials for influencing the kind of programs broadcast. In situations where local initiative programming is possible on certain channels, church leaders need to work together to influence the kinds and quality of programs provided for their community.

Cassette Television

The television cassette is a distinct possibility for the future, even though it is not yet in widespread use by individual viewers. Be alert to developments.

3-D objects

The three-dimensional quality is inherent in many different learning activities for children. See the following categories for specific suggestions involving three-dimensional objects.

Volume 1: Carving, Clay Modeling, Collage, Construction, Diorama.

Volume 2: Mobiles, Models, Paper Sculpture, Papier Mâché.

Volume 3: Sculpture, Stabiles, Wire Sculpture.

time lines

WHAT THEY ARE—

Time lines are a way of visualizing a specific time span and showing the time relationship of certain events within that span. Events are usually arranged along a horizontal line, which serves as the continuum, showing the earliest and latest limits of the time span covered.

Young children will not use this tool because they do not have enough time sense to be able to locate events and people in terms of specific periods in history. As children advance toward the later elementary years, they develop an increasing ability to deal with time concepts. Thus the use of a time line will be more meaningful to older elementary children.

WHEN AND WHERE TO USE THEM—

Children will use time lines most often with units of study that relate to events taking place in various time periods. Time lines will help them to understand the various events that took place in a certain block of time, and the relationships of these events to one another.

Since time lines relate most closely to historical study, children will use them in a classroom setting or in their own personal study.

WHY CHILDREN USE THEM—

Time lines allow children to:
—arrange a series of events in order of occurrence
—see the relationship of events on a time continuum
—arrange in order of occurrence several events in which they have participated (example: rode my bike, stopped at the store, washed my hands, ate my dinner, looked at a book, went to bed); this is a good way to introduce children to time lines
—visualize events occurring on the various days of the week
—visualize sequence of the seasons of the year with appropriate activities related to each
—review the events in a unit of study
—identify the time period when certain historical figures lived
—portray and/or summarize events in the life of biblical or historical characters
—show in detail a group of historical events—the history of a church, a denomination or some other organization
—show the relationship of an event in the past with the present and future
—review the history of another culture.

WHAT CHILDREN NEED—

—lengths of shelf paper or pieces of poster paper, pencils, felt pens, rulers
—materials to make a string or wire time line (eyescrews; wire, clothesline or string; paper clips or clip-type clothespins; colored yarn; small cards or pieces of paper, gummed labels)

HOW TO USE THEM—

Time lines can be simple or complex. In a very simple way, children can attach little boxes to a line by sketching them in with a pencil. Thus, in a moment, they can remind themselves of the time relationships between two persons or events.

More formally, children may want to draw carefully planned time lines so that everyone can use the information. Large pieces of poster paper or lengths of white shelf paper work well. When the time line is sketched in pencil it can be converted with felt pens to a permanent form, with labels marking each part.

An important first step is to mark off the horizontal line in equal segments. Size of the segments can be determined according to the number required and the space available, but be sure to keep them equal. Obviously, the more years involved, the smaller the segments will need to be. Twelve months of one year will come out very differently from a 4000-year period.

On a paper time line, pictures can be drawn to indicate the various events being portrayed; then each picture can be attached to the time line at the correct spot.

An interesting variation is the time line done on string or wire. At a level the children can reach, put eyescrews in place in a wall or woodwork. Stretch a piece of heavy cord or picture wire (or if done outside, clothesline) between the hooks (or use the top of a door hinge and a sturdy nail).

Mark off the string in equal sections identified by paper clips with small labels. Pieces of colored yarn, clip-type clothespins or gummed labels can also be used. Then attach pictures or words on cards to the string to label the persons or events on the time line. One advantage of this variation is that the planning and creating processes (which must be done somewhat separately on paper) are merged here. As the time line is put together, the various items attached to the wire can be adjusted so that the finished product fits together in a unified time sequence.

toys

WHAT THEY ARE—

Toys—objects used by children in play—often are small replicas of everyday objects, such as tools used at home (sweepers, brooms, hammers, pliers, stoves, etc.) and tools used by persons in their work (autos, trucks, typewriters, microscopes, medical kit, etc.).

Emphasis here is placed on a few easily made toys, with instructions. As you search out new toys for children, try to discover the history of your favorites. Check the Bibliography for sources.

WHEN AND WHERE TO USE THEM—

Children enjoy toys in many places, both indoors and outdoors. We naturally associate toys with *play* and *fun,* so children use them at any time and anywhere they are involved in play. Since the suggestions given here each come from a particular culture or part of the world, children might use them in connection with a study of persons and cultures. Toys are not limited to children. Often children and adults can come to a new understanding of each other through sharing a toy.

WHY CHILDREN USE THEM—

Toys allow children to:
—gain skill in manipulating objects
—try on new roles in a "safe" context
—discover new ways to have fun
—grow in motor skills
—understand how children in other cultures play.

WHAT CHILDREN NEED—

—for the hummer: large button and string, or cardboard and crayons or paints

—for the dreidel: heavy construction paper, glue, scissors, felt markers, thin dowel stick or taffy apple stick, hardening clay, dried beans or buttons
—for the bull roarer: thin scraps of wood, felt marker or paint, hand drill, heavy cord

HOW TO MAKE AND USE THEM—

The following simple toys have their origins in other cultures. Children will enjoy knowing about their backgrounds as well as using them.

1. *A Hummer or Spinner.* The origin of this toy is unknown, although American Indian children are known to have used them, along with children in many other parts of the world.

For a very simple hummer, string a large button on a 36-inch piece of cord and knot the ends together. The string must go through two holes in the button (see diagram).

Hold one end of the loop in each hand and begin to spin the button, continuing until the string is wound tightly. Then pull the string and watch the button spin. Sometimes, if you do it rapidly enough, you will hear a humming sound.

You can also make a spinner out of cardboard cut in a circle about 2½ inches in diameter. After punching two holes in the center about 1 inch apart, color interesting designs on both sides of the cardboard. What color can you see when you spin this one? Why? (White, because light is composed of the rainbow of colors.)

2. *Dreidel (pronounced DRAY-dle).* This Hebrew toy is used by children at the Hanukkah festival. A variation is also used by children in the British Isles at Christmas.

The dreidel is a kind of top. Children can make the dreidel in one of two ways:

a. Using heavy construction paper, make a six-sided box (see illustrations).

Cut, fold and glue the paper according to the pattern. Sharpen one end of a thin dowel stick (or taffy apple stick) and push it through the top and bottom of the box as shown. Be sure at least an inch of the stick extends on both ends. Then write the letters

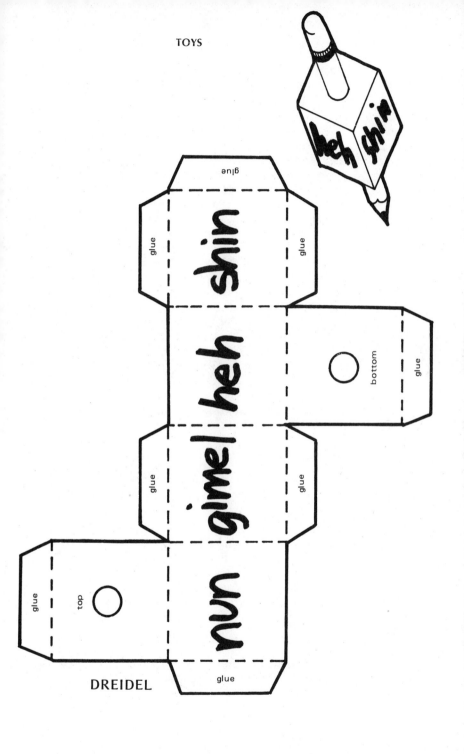

DREIDEL

shown in the diagram on the dreidel with felt marker.

b. An alternative method is to use hardening-type clay for the box. Form the clay around the stick and let it dry. Before it gets too dry, press the letters into the clay with a sharp object.

To play with the dreidel, draw a circle two feet in diameter on cardboard or with chalk on the floor. Give four players an equal number of counters, like ten dried beans or buttons. Decide together how many each person will put into the pot to begin.

Each player takes a turn spinning the dreidel within the circle. If the dreidel stops with "NUN" on top, the player takes all the counters in the pot. If it stops with "GIMEL" up, the player gets half of the pot. If the "HEH" is up, he or she receives nothing. If "SHIN" is up, the player puts a counter into the pot.

Children may be interested to know that each of these is one of the four beginning letters for the words "Nes Gadol Hayak Sham," which mean "A great miracle occurred there."

3. *Bull Roarer.* The bull roarer was used by ancient African tribes, by the Indians of pre-Columbian America, by the people of Tibet, and by the Eskimos of Canada. It should be used outdoors, because it involves spinning a piece of wood overhead. Use a thin scrap of wood about ¼ inch thick, of any size and shape. Encourage children to come up with their own shapes and paint designs with felt markers or paint.

Drill a small hole in the center near one end and tie heavy cord through the hole. The cord should be about 3 or 4 feet long and might have a loop in the other end for the user to slip a finger through.

Spin the roarer as fast as possible overhead and see how the sound of the roaring wind comes and goes.

These suggestions are only starters. Look carefully at the toys that interest your children. Try to find out what makes them special. What do they help the child do? How were they developed?

WHERE TO GET MORE HELP—

Caney, Steven, *Steven Caney's Toy Book.* New York: Workman Publishing Company, 1972. 176 pp. $8.95 (hard) $3.95 (paper)

videotape

WHAT IT IS—

Videotape is a magnetic tape that records both picture and sound track. The recording is played back through the videotape recorder, with the video portion visible over a television monitor or screen while the audio portion is played back through the television monitor's sound speaker. Most videotape equipment for nonprofessionals at present requires either ½-inch or 1-inch tape format, while equipment used by commercial television studios takes a 2-inch format. This lack of compatibility creates difficulties for church use.

WHEN TO USE IT—

Children can use videotape whenever the videotape recorder, its camera and a playback monitor are available. They can use this equipment when they wish to record both sound and picture images for later reproduction.

WHERE TO USE IT—

Children can use videotape almost anywhere if they have access to a portable videotape recorder. These are battery operated and light enough for an adult to carry from place to place. If children have access only to an electrically powered videotape recorder, they will have to use it where it can be plugged in. This could be in any classroom situation or outdoor setting where an electric power source is available.

WHY CHILDREN USE IT—

Videotape allows children to:
—make their own audio and video recordings of almost anything
—preserve for later use both visual and sound images

—experiment with the manipulation of a videotape camera and gain experience in recording the kind of visual images they want to record

—record for later critiquing puppet performances, plays and dramas, creative movement and pantomime, thus using videotape as a means of improving performance in one of these skills

—have fun experimenting with the combined recording of both sight and sound.

WHAT CHILDREN NEED—

—a videotape camera, recorder and playback monitor

—blank videotape in the proper size

—instructions on how to use the videotape recorder

—freedom with supervision to experiment and gain confidence in use of the equipment

—lots of good ideas on what to record

—*A Word About Compatibility:* At present, one technical problem is that recorders of various types and various brands are not compatible. That is, material recorded on one recorder will not always play back properly on another, even if the two are of the same type and/or brand. Recordings made on ½-inch tape will not play back on 1-inch machines and vice versa. At present, most educators using videotape are experimenting creatively with their own equipment and playing the tapes back on their own machines.

HOW TO USE IT—

It is very important that children learn the basic rules for using videotape equipment. Once these guidelines have been made clear, children should be able to handle the equipment and produce some creative recordings. Be sure they understand that videotape equipment is very sensitive and must be kept in good working order. With a few ground rules about what children can and cannot do, boys and girls can take good care of this equipment.

Note: Be sure to have adults train the children, but these persons should not be so possessive of the equipment that they are unable to let the children have some freedom within certain limits.

Using the Recorder

Once the equipment's operation has been explained, children should have lots of time to experiment by recording persons and objects around them in the room. They need to get the feel of the equipment before they try to record anything they really want to preserve. Emphasize that they should think about the special things they can do with the videotape recorder that they cannot do with their audio tape recorder. Ask, "What is special about this, so that you need to get a picture of it as well as the sound of it?" Try to get the children to think about both the picture and the sound they will be recording simultaneously.

Since the microphone will probably remain in one position (unless you have lapel mikes for each person), operation of the camera will take the most practice.

Some Possible Recordings

The following is a beginning list of recordings children might want to make.

1. *Reports.* Any kind of committee report, sharing or demonstration might be recorded on videotape, especially if special visual effects are used—a map, some charts, or a demonstration of how to do something, such as making candles or doing paper sculpture. Help the boys and girls think through what they want people to see as well as hear.

2. *Plays, Dramas, Pantomimes.* Almost any dramatic presentation lends itself to videotape recording, since the movement of the players is of great importance, whether or not there are spoken words.

3. *Interviews.* An interview could be videotaped if the person had some special characteristic that could best be demonstrated (such as a hobby or collection being shared) or if the person had to be interviewed when the children could not be present. An example would be an interview with an old person who had to be interviewed at home where it was not possible for all the children to be present.

4. *Movement or Dance.* Preserve special movements or dance steps to share later with others.

5. *Worship.* Record a typical or special worship experience being shared by boys and girls if there is a reason to preserve it for some later use.

weaving

WHAT IT IS—

Weaving—the interlacing of threads or strips of material into flat pieces or into shaped pieces like a basket—has been used since early humans learned to put leaves together to make shelter. People have always used what was available—reeds and grasses; wool and later cotton threads; synthetics and now the new polyesters.

For example, American Indians wove blankets, rugs, baskets and other everyday items. They used natural materials and vegetable dyes, yielding such colors as brown, black, gray and white. Designs were memorized and passed from mother to daughter.

There are many different types of weaving. A simple design similar to the spider's web is the Mexican Eye of God design (p. 99) on two sticks, using wool yarns and done without a loom. Other methods use simple looms or more complex hand- and machine-operated types. The process is basically the same for all types of weaving, but here we will deal with the simpler forms.

WHEN AND WHERE TO DO IT—

Children can enjoy weaving when they wish to create beautiful designs with threads, yarns, or reeds and grasses. This might be when they are studying the weaving (or other creations) of different cultures, or it might be done simply as a creative expression.

Weaving can be done anywhere by children, since the materials are movable.

WHY CHILDREN DO IT—

Weaving allows children to:
—explore the use of thread, yarns, etc. in woven designs
—discover for themselves an age-old technique for making one large object out of many small ones
—develop designs in simple flat weaving.

WHAT CHILDREN NEED—

—materials for weaving:
yarns (solid color or variegated, for knitting or for rugs)
ribbons
seine cord or macrame cords
sea grasses
reeds
raffia
strips of polyester cloth (1 inch wide)
square or rectangular sections of plastic or twine mesh bags used in packaging fruits and vegetables
—various types of looms:
cardboard loom (8 by 10 or 10 by 12-inch heavy cardboard or a circle of cardboard)
frame loom (picture frame, canvas stretcher or wood strips 1 by 2 inches or as large as you want it)
hardware cloth or chicken wire (12 by 15-inch size or smaller)
—other supplies: ruler, pencil, large blunt needle or tapestry needle, large tooth comb, bamboo skewer or tongue depressors, pieces of dowel rod or smooth twigs

HOW TO DO IT—

Each of the following sections gives instructions for a different weaving project that children might like to try.

1. *Mesh Weaving.* Even young children can make loosely woven designs using plastic or twine mesh bags in which potatoes, onions, grapefruit and oranges are often packaged. Each bag provides at least two good-sized pieces of mesh which could be cut into smaller sizes, if necessary. Let the children

use a coarse rug yarn, ribbon or raffia. To fix one end for weaving, twist it and wrap a small piece of masking tape around it. Let the children create their own designs by going in and out of the holes in the mesh.

2. *Chicken Wire Weaving.* For another simple weaving project for young children, cut chicken wire or hardware cloth into various sizes and cover the edges with masking tape or staple into a frame of 1 by 2-inch pieces of wood. Children can use the designs in the wire and add their own ideas, weaving in and out as they wish. Narrow strips of polyester fabric are bright and colorful for this simple type of weaving.

3. *Mexican Eye of God Symbol.* Form a cross with two pieces of ¼-inch dowel rod or smooth twigs by lashing them together at the center with colored yarn. Then begin winding yarn in a clockwise direction from one rod to the next. At each rod, cross over the front of the stick, making one turn around and behind, before going on to the next stick. When you come to the end of a piece of yarn, knot it off at the next stick and start a new piece at the same point. New colors can be started at any time in the same way. Keep winding around the sticks in a clockwise direction until the design is as large as you want it to be. To add tassels at the outside corners of the weaving on the horizontal rod, cut 12-inch pieces of yarn, making sure that you include all the colors used in the design. Wrap all pieces around the dowel rod at the middle point of the 12-inch length and tie tightly with a knot, thus making a 6-inch tassel on each side.

4. *Finger Weaving* (without a loom). To make a strip of woven material, you need six pieces of yarn 18 inches long and a dowel rod or smooth twig. Tie each piece of yarn to the rod six inches from one end of the yarn, leaving six 12-inch pieces hanging loose. Knot the 6-inch pieces together near the end and secure so that tension can be put on the yarn by pulling on the other end. The knot can be put in a drawer, over a doorknob or drawer pull, or over a hook (see illustration).

MEXICAN EYE OF
GOD SYMBOL

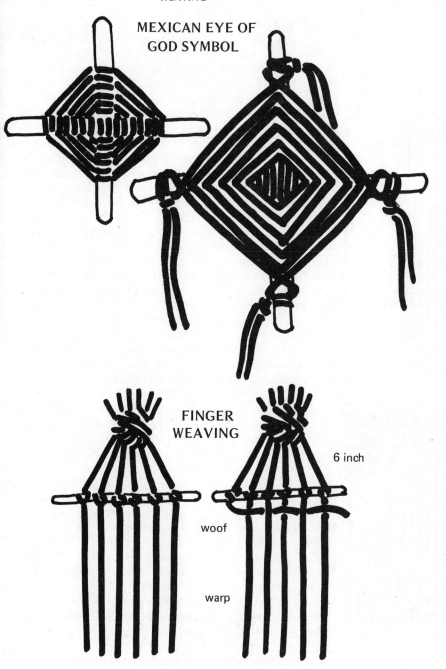

FINGER
WEAVING

6 inch

woof

warp

The weaving is done on the 12-inch pieces of yarn still hanging from the dowel rod. The piece farthest to the left of the weaver is the piece (the woof) that will be woven over and under the other five pieces (the warp). For the first row, go over and under through all five warp pieces. For row two, the weaver must come back in the opposite direction, making sure to get the yarn being woven (the woof) around the first piece of warp when starting back. This will put each row of woof opposite to the one preceding it; that is, if the woof yarn went over one of the warp pieces on the previous row, it must go under on this row, and so forth. Keep pushing the weaving yarn (woof) up toward the dowel rod so that the woven part stays together and fairly tight. You will begin to see the over-and-under pattern emerge. Continue weaving until the design is six inches from the end of the 12-inch pieces. During this process, you will probably need to add woof pieces by knotting on another piece of yarn before continuing.

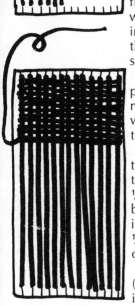

When the weaving is finished, tie off the 6-inch fringe at both ends. At the end where you finished weaving, knot in pairs the end pieces of yarn, leaving one single piece in the middle. At the end with the dowel rod, first untie the large knot securing all six pieces and then tie off the pieces in pairs.

Length can be varied by the length of the warp pieces you begin with. Width can be varied by the number of pieces you begin with, so long as you always have an even number of pieces and use one of them for weaving.

5. *Cardboard Looms.* Make a simple loom by cutting a piece of heavy cardboard about one inch larger than the size of the woven object planned. Mark off ¼-inch spaces along two opposite sides of the cardboard (the top and bottom), choosing the short sides if your cardboard is rectangular. For heavy yarn, use ½-inch spaces. Then make a ¼-inch-deep cut at each of the lines you have marked.

To put in the threads that will run up and down (the warp threads), make a knot in the yarn about 3 inches from the end and slide the knot into the first cut at the top. Wind down the front of the cardboard, slipping the yarn through the first cut at the bottom. Come up the back of the cardboard to the second cut, and slip yarn through the cut. Continue winding up and down, around the cardboard, moving each time to the next cut and covering both front and back of the cardboard with warp threads. Do not pull the yarn too tight. Place a knot in the yarn after slipping it through the last cut, and leave a 5-inch tail.

To weave horizontally, thread a blunt needle with yarn (woof thread). Begin weaving horizontally *over* the first thread and *under* the next thread, continuing all the way across. Do not pull your yarn too tight or the cardboard will buckle and bend. When you turn to go back for the second row of weaving, be sure to go around the last warp thread so that your next row will be exactly the opposite from the previous one. Where you went over, you will now go under. Each time you reverse directions, go around the last thread before starting back. Continue until you have gone as far as you can go. This is known as the Tabby Weave or plain weave pattern (over one and under one strand).

Beating: If you want a close weave, push the woof thread tightly up against the previous row with a ruler or comb. This is called beating or bubbling the woof.

Note: Be very careful not to run your needle through a piece of the warp yarn as you go over and under. This will cause it to split and come apart more quickly.

If you wish, you can experiment as you go with other patterns—over two and under two, over two and under one, over three and under two, etc.

To finish, you must work in the loose ends left as you finished each piece of yarn. Do this by threading up the end and working it in along the edge of the weaving.

To remove the weaving from the cardboard, cut the warp threads running along the back of the cardboard at about the center. This will give you some long end pieces for fringe. Tie them together, first in pairs and then in fours, and shorten to an appropriate length.

6. *Round Cardboard Loom.* Children can use the

same technique to make a round hot pad with a cardboard base. Make two 8-inch circles of cardboard, and cut out a 1½-inch round hole at the center. Two circles are used to strengthen the cardboard. Measure around the outside edge of the cardboard pieces, putting a mark every ½ inch, making certain that you have an uneven number of marks. Then make ¼-inch cuts into the double thickness of cardboard. Using heavy rug yarn, thread the warp threads by going around and around the cardboard from front to back. This warp thread goes through the large center hole and then slips through each cut around the outside edge. The ends of the warp yarn can be secured with a dab of white glue. Now begin weaving the woof thread at the inside edge and weave in and out, going around and around and working your way toward the outer edge of the circle. Children can experiment with different patterns as they go, using several weaving designs. Finish by slipping one or more pieces of yarn underneath the warp threads to conceal the rough edge of the cardboard.

7. *Frame Loom.* A frame loom uses the same process as described for cardboard, except that a wooden frame with rows of finishing nails across two ends provides the tension in the warp threads needed to do the weaving. Mark off spaces for an even number of nails and allow enough space at each side to provide working room at the edges. Then wind the warp yarn around the nails, going from top to bottom instead of around the back as you did with the cardboard loom. Weave the woof thread as above.

wire sculpture

WHAT IT IS—

Wire sculpture is the creation of three-dimensional designs, objects and figures by bending, shaping and twisting wire. Children can best design wire sculpture to stand on a flat surface, although it is also possible to design hanging sculptures.

WHEN AND WHERE TO DO IT—

Children can do wire sculpture at any time and in any place, as long as they have the necessary materials.

WHY CHILDREN DO IT—

Wire sculpture allows children to:
—increase their manual dexterity
—create an artistic design fairly easily and quickly
—work with a medium that allows them to make many decisions about what to do next, which direction or shape to use and when it is finished
—experiment with elements of balance and design as they create new shapes
—experiment with art forms that may or may not represent something.

WHAT CHILDREN NEED—

—lots of good ideas about what they would like to create
—wire (16- or 18-gauge wire is fairly flexible but firm; other possibilities include bailing wire, stovepipe wire, florists' wire, coat hanger wire, telephone cable wire; try to get some in different colors, e.g. aluminum and copper, multicolored telephone wire)
—pliers (with wire cutter)
—base (optional)

HOW TO DO IT—

Here are some simple steps for children to follow:
1. Get an idea! It will be helpful if children have some ideas with which to begin. "I'm going to make a horse!" is one idea; "I'm going to make something tall and twisty!" is another. The ideas may or may not represent some object, animal or person and may even be as simple as "round" or "long."

If you are using wire sculpture with a particular unit of study, you may want to suggest illustrating things you have been learning about. Wire sculpture can be used to make simple versions of homes, dolls, masks, etc., but do not force your children to use wire to reproduce something that could better be done in another medium. Remember that the wire best lends itself to forming light and open creations.

2. Experiment with wire. Each piece has different qualities. Coat hanger wire is very stiff and hard to shape; telephone wire is easy to bend and colorful. Some wire is better for the main body or central part of a form, while other wire is more useful when attached to the main figure by twisting. Let the children discover these qualities by experimenting. *Note:* Always have coat hanger wire untwisted at the hook; you may or may not want to cut off the twisted section before the children begin to work with it.

3. Let the children create! Trust them to come up with their own ideas. They are full of them. Let them discover what will balance and what will not, which wire will support the weight and which will not. Encourage them to try new ideas and to share ideas.

4. Variations:

—Wire sculpture can be used alone or decorated with yarn, string, plaster (molded onto the wire), melted wax (dripped onto the wire), papier mâché (strips molded either directly onto the wire or over crumpled paper stuffed between wires).

—Show children how they can achieve new shapes by twisting and wrapping wire around fingers, pencils, rulers, other objects.

—Help children learn how to attach pieces of wire to each other by twisting with pliers.

—See also Mobiles (Volume 2) and Stabiles.

wood

Wood, a natural fiber, is one of the earth's most versatile materials and is common in some form in all of the world's cultures. Wood can be cut into many thicknesses and shapes. It can be bent when wet. It can be carved and painted. It can also be glued, and its surfaces can be decorated in many ways.

All children can work with wood, and younger children should be given every opportunity to do so. They can learn to handle carpentry tools (see Carpentry, Volume I), and they can make constructions out of a variety of shapes, colors and sizes of wood pieces (see Construction, Volume 1). They can form collages on sawn slabs of wood (see Collage, Volume I), and they can paint on wood. Older children can carve wood (see Carving, Volume 1). They can use cuts of logs or gracefully shaped tree limbs to form bases for string designs (see String) or wire sculpture (see Wire Sculpture). Or they can make a toy (see "Bull Roarer" in Toys).

As children work with wood, help them to appreciate its properties as well as its beauty.

worship

WHAT IT IS—

Worship for children is the expression, either formal or informal, of their relationship with God. This relationship changes constantly for boys and girls, but it is always rooted in the reality of their personal experiences. Worship that does not express the way things are now will not be meaningful to children. Worship may take many forms, involving use of the arts (music, painting, sculpture, architecture, drama, etc.) as well as words (poetry, readings, Bible use, sharing of thoughts and feelings, etc.).

The following sections are related to this discussion and should also be consulted: Banners and Choral Reading, Volume 1; Litany, Movement, Music and Poetry, Volume 2.

WHEN TO DO IT—

Worship can take place either privately or in a group. Within a class group, worship will take place at different times. With younger children it will often occur spontaneously when children and leaders express their relationship with God as a result of something they have just seen or heard or done. With older children, worship will more often be a planned time when children and leaders focus their attention on God and their relationship with God. Again, these worship moments will be related to common experiences in the lives of the children in the group. Private worship will occur whenever children are led to express their own feelings about God.

WHERE TO DO IT—

Informal and private worship can occur anywhere, including church, home, neighborhood and school.

More formal group worship will usually be planned as part of a class session to take place either indoors or outdoors. Since all children are in the process of learning *about* worship and learning *to* worship, careful attention should be given to the surroundings used for worship experiences. Surroundings should contribute to learning rather than detract from it.

WHY CHILDREN DO IT—

Children worship to:
—learn more about their own and others' understanding of God
—experience various forms through which our relationship with God can be expressed
—sense the common bond that draws together those who worship God
—discover what others have done (through music, art, the Bible, poetry, etc.) to express their relationship with God, and to share in that expression
—deepen their own personal relationship with God.

WHAT CHILDREN NEED—

—opportunities to think about what worship is and to experience it, both formally and informally, in ways appropriate for their age

106

—worship materials suitable for children (songs and hymns, prayers, Bible passages and stories, stories from other sources, choral readings and litanies, drama and movement, poems, pictures, etc.)
—opportunity to gain experience in planning and leading worship

HOW TO DO IT—

Ways Children Worship

Children should be guided naturally into experiences of private worship so that they will become accustomed to such moments. In class groups leaders can make such times a part of the regular plan, especially among older children. For example, a church school classroom can have a special place arranged for private worship, where boys and girls may pray, read the Bible, think quietly or enjoy a picture or object from God's creation. A day camp session in the outdoors could have a built-in time for each person to be alone with their feelings about God. Be sure to provide specific suggestions and helps as necessary for the age of your children.

Group worship may be spontaneous and informal or planned and formal.

Spontaneous worship will occur among children of all ages, and is most often related directly to something the group has been doing. This type of worship predominates among young children who cannot yet manage detailed planning and implementation necessary for a more formal service. When two kindergarten children stop arguing over who gets to use a particular truck and begin to work together, building roadways and delivering things in the truck, their teacher may lead them and other children nearby into worship by using the Bible verse "Love one another" (John 15:17), either as spoken words or as a song, and by praying a brief prayer of thanks for friends. This will probably take no more than two or three minutes. Yet it will occur in the context of an experience that is fresh in the children's lives, and it will express this restored relationship between two children in terms of our own relationship with God. As young children gain experience in such brief periods of worship they will increase in their ability to express their relationship with God through full participation in a group with other children.

Teachers of older children, too, need constantly to be on the alert for moments when boys and girls can stop to express thanks or praise for events that have just occurred. Increasingly, older children can participate by contributing to such informal moments of worship.

Planned worship is also likely to be tied directly to certain events in the life of a group—the climax of a particular session, the close of a unit of study. As much as ability and interest will permit, older boys and girls should be directly involved in planning and carrying out such services. These need not be lengthy, but they should be full of involvement for the children. Plans should include much active participation by group members. Leaders should make available various possibilities that will relate to whatever theme is being followed. Worship materials that have already been created or used by the children in their class sessions should be used again. If children have written a litany or studied a hymn, be sure to use these. If they have learned a particular Bible passage, include it. Planned worship should relate directly to experiences that all the children have in common.

Children will often be involved in family worship. Parents may help their children learn how to have regular periods of private prayer and worship. Family worship may also be a group experience, as the entire family gathers at mealtimes, or in regular family devotional periods or special family celebrations.

Some Guidelines to Remember

As you help children learn about worship, keep in mind these guidelines:

1. *Location will vary.* Worship can happen anywhere. It should take place in a spot related to what has been happening with the children. Location should be determined in part by the purposes of worship in relation to the children's other experiences.

2. *Timing will vary.* When worship occurs will be determined by how it fits into a total schedule, as well

as how it relates to children's other experiences.

3. *Ways worship is carried out will vary.* Sometimes children and leaders will be seated on the floor in a circle, or on a rug, or outside under a tree. At other times rows of chairs facing a worship center will be appropriate. Sometimes spontaneous participation will be desirable. At other times there will be a planned order of service.

4. *Worship must be related to children's experiences.* Make worship relate directly to the important things in children's lives now.

5. *Worship must be related to children's age level and interest.* Select materials that can be easily understood. Don't allow a worship experience to be too long.

6. *All worship materials must help children express or experience their relationship with God.* Evaluate a song, hymn, prayer, or reading from this perspective. Some popular music, art or other materials, otherwise useful, may not be appropriate for worship.

writing

WHAT IT IS—

Writing involves organizing ideas, thoughts and information, and putting them on paper. Fiction is stories that are true to life but did not actually happen. Story writing involves organizing persons (characters), places (setting) and events (plot) into a connected sequence. Nonfiction writing requires organizing information, ideas and thoughts on certain subjects.

As young children begin to verbalize their thoughts, they often write by dictating to another person who writes down what they have said and reads it back to them. They can also dictate into a tape recorder. Older children can increase their verbal skills by creating fantasy worlds or describing real events on paper.

WHEN TO DO IT—

Children write when they are interested in capturing in semi-permanent form what they have been saying or thinking. In this section we include letter-writing, diaries or logbooks, invitations, personal reflections (essays), fantasy and story writing. Other writing experiences are described in Newspaper, Poetry and Playwriting (Volume 2).

Writing can be used to capture special times in a child's life—sending a message through the mail as a letter to a friend; recording personal reflections on an event in their life; capturing in words their own imaginings; putting together persons, places and events to create a story of their own.

Writing is often appropriate just after children have had some new experience—a trip to a new place or an opportunity to talk with some new person.

WHERE TO DO IT—

Writing can be done anywhere that children can get a pencil and paper and jot down their ideas or a tape recorder to talk into.

WHY CHILDREN DO IT—

Children write in order to:
—experience recording their own ideas
—bring together real world events and their own imaginations
—learn the power ot words to convey messages
—increase their own power of abstract thinking
—share part of themselves with other persons in other places
—discover their own creative skill in using words
—discover the fun of creating the necessary elements for a story: imaginary people, places and events.

WHAT CHILDREN NEED—

—lined paper and pencils
—tape recorder (especially for younger children)
—large blocks of uninterrupted time
—adult leaders who:
spur ideas with a few key words, questions or word games

encourage children to try capturing their immediate feelings or ideas

help children develop trust in their own abilities and thinking processes

stimulate children to do the best they can

—Note: Children need to know that they can write about things with which they are familiar. At first they should not try to write about the ocean if they have never been there. As their abilities grow they will be able to use information and ideas they have gained through their own reading. This comes gradually, through maturity.

—Note: Children need constant assurance that what they produce will be acceptable right now.

HOW TO DO IT—

Young children can get their first experience in putting thoughts and ideas together with adults serving as scribes. Encourage the child to "talk out" his or her ideas as you write them down, and then read them back. Four- or five-year-olds are thrilled to have their own stories read back to them or displayed on a bulletin board.

With young children this is the beginning of extending their thinking about a particular subject from three sentences about a boat to a complete story about a boat ride down the river. Some persons like to use the tape recorder to encourage children to verbalize. As the child's thinking patterns develop, words come much faster than they can be written down. The tape recorder can catch them for later transcription.

Older children are better able to talk through and test their ideas with other persons before writing them down, building confidence in their creations.

Children should be encouraged to write down their ideas as they get them. They should not worry about the use or even spelling of particular words. If they first get the story or ideas down naturally, later they can reread, work on spelling and punctuation, and prepare the final version for use in the group or in a display.

Hints to Teachers: Writing should be only one alternative for self-expression. Some children will choose to put their thoughts and ideas in words on paper, while others will express them in clay or paint. Do not force all children to write, but be certain that writing materials are available and that it is one alternative for creative expression.

Display writing as you would a picture. Mount it on colored paper; place it in a display or on the bulletin board. Encourage children to read their own material to others in the group.

Here are some starters to stimulate children to write. Ask questions about a picture: What is happening here? Who is involved? What may happen next? Ask questions about an event: What did you see? Who was there? How did they look? What were they doing? What did they say? What did you do? Ask questions about feelings: What was your reaction? How did you feel inside? What did it make you think of? What did it make you want to do next?

Possible Writing Projects

1. *Letters.* Draw a diagram to show how a letter is arranged and what its parts are, but emphasize ideas to include rather than form. Children can tell of their activities, include photos, newspaper pictures and pictures they have drawn. They can include picture postcards and describe places they have visited. They can ask questions about the activities of a friend in another place and find out what kinds of things that person enjoys. They can find out what it is like where that person lives. Help children think of letters as conversations on paper. Encourage them to think of things they would like to tell the person to whom they are writing, as well as things they would like to ask.

2. *Invitations.* Children can make attractive invitations simply by folding a plain 4 by 6-inch index card once, making a 4 by 3-inch invitation.

They can create their own design for the front of the card and write their invitation on the inside.

Be sure the children include such information as the following on their invitations:

112

To ————————————(what event)
When ——————————(date)
Where ——————————(address)
Time ——————————(beginning and ending time)
RSVP ——————————(give phone number
or address so persons
can tell you if they
are able to attend)

a birthday Party

3. *Diary or Log Book*. The purpose of keeping a diary is to record events, ideas, thoughts, and what you have seen and done. Some older children may want to keep a daily diary, but for many children the idea works best if done for a shorter period—for example, a diary kept on a certain trip, noting places seen or visited, people met, unusual events or experiences. A log book might be kept as part of a certain study, such as one on an ecology emphasis entitled, "Pollution I Have Seen." Facts could be gathered for a certain period of time and then reported back to the group or to an environmental agency.

A simple notebook or a few pages stapled together make an ideal short-term log book.

4. *Personal Reflections*. This is a highly personal kind of writing in which the child expresses his or her ideas about something. Emphasize the value of the child's ideas. Children are thinking now as children, and writing their ideas down is one way of affirming the worth of their present thinking.

To stimulate children's thinking, encourage them to think and write about such ideas as:
"The thing I most wish would happen is . . ."
"I feel that . . ."
"I hope to . . ."
"I think most often about . . ."
"If I could go to . . . I would like to . . ."
"We can live in peace if . . ."
These personal thoughts can vary from a few words to a complete essay. Let the length be determined by the extent of the child's ideas.

5. *Fantasy*. Imaginative writing allows children to be especially creative with their word pictures and images. Stimulate this kind of writing with questions like these: If you could be someone or something else, what would you be? Where would you like to go? What does it look like there? Who else is there? What do you do there?

6. *Story Writing*. Children will often want to tell part of their story aloud before beginning to write it down as a way of testing their ideas. Often the written story will change a great deal from the first oral

telling, but this is part of the process of evolving a good story. The written version is in effect a rewrite of the oral story. If a child tells the story first he or she will have the entire story in mind and know where it goes and how it comes out in the end. This is a helpful perspective from which to begin perfecting the story later on paper.

Some Pointers: As children progress with their writing skills, it is often helpful to encourage them to think of the A-B-C-Ds of short story writing:

A—action that makes the story

B—background in which the action takes place

C—characters

D—dialogue that makes the characters come alive and helps tell about them.

Several additional suggestions may be helpful: The story should have only a small number of characters. These characters and their events should take place over a short time span, so the action is limited to a few incidents. The story can be funny, sad or scary. Such stories are often told in the third person (he, she) and sometimes in the first person (I). Use colorful words that create pictures in the reader's mind.

A Word Game to Encourage Story Creation: Give each child three words (often nouns) and ask them to weave the words into an oral story. Examples would be:

parent, box, birthday

cookie, glass, chair

cat, yarn, newspaper

horse, trail, police

Jesus, sick man, boat

Japan, blossom, Mt. Fuji

One rule is that the three words actually have to be used in the story. Unlimited word combinations can be the stimulus for many creative stories.

other volumes in this series

The other two volumes in this series contain the following learning activities:

VOLUME 1

Acting Out/Drama
Banners
Beads
Books and Stories
Cameras
Candles
Carpentry
Carving
Casting
Charts
Choral Reading

Clay Modeling
Collage
Collecting
Construction
Conversation/
    Discussion
Crayons
Decoupage
Diorama
Dolls
Drawing

Dyeing
Exhibit
Felt Pens
Field Trips
Films and Film-
    strips
Flannel Boards
Foods
Games
Glass
Interview

VOLUME 2

Jewelry
Kites
Lettering
Litany
Macramé
Maps and Globes
Masks
Metal
Mobiles
Models
Montage

Mosaic
Motion Pictures
Movement
Mural
Music
Nature
Newspaper
Overhead
    Projection
Painting
Paper

Papier Mâché
Pictures
Plaques
Plastics
Playwriting
Poetry
Posters
Pottery
Prints & Printing
Puppets
Puzzles

bibliography

Allstrom, Elizabeth. *Let's Play a Story*. New York: Friendship Press, 1966. (Creative dramatics)

Alkema, Chester Jay. *The Complete Crayon Book*. New York: Sterling Publishing Company, Inc., 1969. (Wide variety of crayon projects)

Benarde, Anita. *Games from Many Lands*. New York: The Lion Press, Inc., 1971. (Games)

Benson, Dennis. *Gaming*. Nashville: Abingdon Press, 1971. (How to create simulations)

Bernstein, Marion H. *Off Loom Weaving*. New York: Sterling Publishing Company, Inc., 1971. (Weaving)

The Camera Cookbook (#BA003-3). Watertown, Mass. 02172: Workshop for Learning Things, Inc., 5 Bridge Street, 1970. (Step-by-step manual on photography for children)

Caney, Steven. *Steven Caney's Toy Book*. New York: Workman Publishing Company, 1972. (Toys to make)

Carlson, Bernice Wells. *Let's Pretend It Happened to You*. Nashville: Abingdon Press, 1973. (Stories for creative dramatics)

Carlson, Elliot. *Learning Through Games*. Washington, D.C.: Public Affairs Press, 1970. (Survey of simulation/gaming)

Comins, Jeremy. *Latin American Crafts and Their Cultural Backgrounds*. New York: Lothrop, Lee and Shepard Company, 1974. (Authentic designs and projects in metal, cloth and wood)

Coskey, Evelyn. *Easter Eggs for Everyone*. Nashville: Abingdon Press, 1973. (History of the Easter egg and decorating suggestions)

Cross, Jeanne. *Simple Printing Methods*. New York: S. G. Phillips, Inc., 1972. (Simple descriptions of the printing process)

D'Amato, Janet and Alex. *African Crafts for You to Make*. New York: Julian Messner (div. of Simon & Schuster), 1969. (Background of African culture plus authentic craft designs)

————————————. *Indian Crafts*. New York: The Lion Press, Inc., 1968. (Background of American Indian culture plus craft designs)

Downer, Marion. *Kites: How to Make and Fly Them*. New York: Lothrop, Lee and Shepard Company, 1968. (Easy-to-follow instructions)

Eisenberg, Helen and Larry. *The New Pleasure Chest*. Nashville: Abingdon Press, 1972. (Games)

Ellison, Elsie C. *Fun With Lines and Curves*. New York: Lothrop, Lee and Shepard Company, 1972. (String figures)

Engstrom, W. A. *Multi-media in the Church: A Beginner's Guide for Putting It All Together*. Richmond, Va.: John Knox Press, 1973. (Technical aspects of production of visuals and sound)

Gregg, Elizabeth M. *What To Do When There's Nothing To Do*. New York: Dell, 1970. (Play activities for young children)

Glubok, Shirley. *The Art of Japan.* New York: Macmillan, 1970. (Culture and the arts. Note: Look for some thirty other books by the same author, including books on certain countries, on archeology, on Bible lands, and on American colonial days and American Indians.)

Helfman, Harry. *Making Your Own Sculpture.* New York: William Morrow and Company, 1971. (Sculpture in various media, including dough, straws, wire, etc.)

Hoke, John. *Terrariums.* New York: Franklin Watts, Inc., 1972. (Environments in glass containers)

Horvath, Joan. *Filmmaking for Beginners.* New York: Thomas Nelson, Inc., 1974. (Children using film)

Howard, Sylvia W. *Tin-Can Crafting.* New York: Sterling Publishing Company, Inc., 1971. (Recycling tin)

Hunt, Kari and Bernice Carlson. *Masks and Mask Makers.* Nashville: Abingdon Press, 1961. (Making and using masks)

Ickis, Marguerite and Reba Esh. *The Book of Arts and Crafts.* New York: Dover, 1973. (Reprint of a classic crafts book)

Jones, G. William. *Landing Rightside Up in TV and Film.* Nashville: Abingdon Press, 1973. (Utilization of media)

Joseph, Joan. *Folk Toys Around the World and How To Make Them.* New York: Parents' Magazine Press, 1972. (Toys to make; also includes history)

Krinsky, Norman. *Art for City Children.* New York: Van Nostrand Reinhold, 1970. (Art projects for classroom and home use)

"Learning Resource Filing System" (Pamphlet #426-E). Nashville, TN 37202: Cokesbury Church Library Service, 201 Eighth Avenue, South. (Provides categories for filing pictures, filmstrips, charts, maps, etc.)

McGuirk, Donn P. *Better Media for Less Money.* Scottsdale, Arizona 85253: National Teacher Education Project, 6947 E. MacDonald Drive, 1972. (Plans for teaching equipment)

Meyer, Carolyn. *Saw, Hammer and Paint: Woodworking and Finishing for Beginners.* New York: William Morrow and Company, 1973. (Carpentry skills and projects)

Millen, Nina. *Children's Festivals from Many Lands.* New York: Friendship Press, 1964. (Religious and folk festivals arranged by continents)

—————————. *Children's Games from Many Lands.* New York: Friendship Press, 1969. (All types of games from world cultures)

Munson, Don and Allianora Rosse. *The Paper Book: 187 Things to Make.* New York: Charles Scribner's Sons, 1972. (Basic book on paper activities)

Murray, William D. and Francis J. Rigney. *Paper Folding for Beginners.* New York: Dover, n.d. (Introduction to Origami)

Musselman, Virginia. *Learning About Nature Through Crafts.* Harrisburg, Pa.: Stackpole Books, 1969. (Many uses for nature materials)

Newman, Thelma R. et al. *Paper As Art and Craft.* New York: Crown Publishers, Inc., 1973. (Multi-uses of paper)

Newsome, Arden J. *Candles: A Step by Step Guide to Creative Candlemaking.* New York: Lancer Books, 1972. (Basic candlemaking processes)

—————————. *Crafts and Toys From Around the World.* New York: Julian

Messner (div. of Simon & Schuster), 1972. (American toys from other cultures)

Paul, Aileen and Arthur Hawkins. *Kids Cooking: A First Cookbook for Children.* New York: Pocket Books, 1971. (Beginning cooking)

Post, Henry and Michael McTwigan. *Clay Play: Learning Games for Children.* Englewood Cliffs, N.J.: Prentice Hall, Inc., 1973. (Basic discoveries in clay)

Pringle, Laurence. *Ecology: Science of Survival.* New York: Macmillan Company, 1971. (Interrelatedness of environments)

Purdy, Susan. *Festivals for You To Celebrate.* Philadelphia: J. B. Lippincott and Company, 1969. (Origins of festivals and related craft projects)

—————————. *Jewish Holidays: Facts, Crafts and Activities.* Philadelphia: J. B. Lippincott and Company, 1969. (Jewish festivals)

Rackow, Leo. *Postercraft.* New York: Sterling Publishing Company, Inc., 1971. (Techniques for making posters, including use of felt pens)

Rynew, Arden. *Motion Picture Production Handbook.* Dayton, Ohio: Pflaum/Standard Publishing Company, 1971. (Filmmaking)

St. Tamara. *Asian Crafts.* New York: The Lion Press, Inc., 1970. (Forms of Asian design in many projects)

Sargent, Lucy. *Tin Craft for Christmas.* New York: William Morrow and Company, 1969. (Excellent designs for tin cans)

Schrank, Jeffrey. *Using Games in Religion Class.* Paramus, N.J.: Paulist Press, 1973. (Identifies a variety of simulations for religion classes)

Segal, Jo Ahern. *Dye-Craft: A Guide to the Ancient and Contemporary Skills of Solid-dye, Tie-dye, Fold-dye, Block-dye, Pour-on Dye, and Batik.* Coventry, Connecticut 06238: Educational Aids, Box 307. (Step-by-step instructions for the dyeing process)

Seidelman, James E. and Grace Mintonye. *Creating Mosaics.* New York: Crowell-Collier Press, 1967. (Details for paper, food and pebble mosaics)

—————————————————. *Creating With Clay.* New York: Crowell-Collier Press, 1967. (Urges children to discover ways to use clay)

—————————————————. *The Rub Book.* New York: Macmillan, 1968. (One boy's discoveries in rubbings)

Sharp, Evelyn. *Thinking Is Child's Play.* New York: Avon, 1970. (Games for use at home or school based on Jean Piaget's theories of cognitive development)

Siks, Geraldine. *Children's Literature for Dramatization.* New York: Harper and Brothers, 1964. (A classic in world literature)

Sommer, Joellen with Elyse Sommer. *Sew Your Own Accessories.* New York: Lothrop, Lee and Shepard Company, 1972. (Gifts and room accessories to make)

Sperling, Walter. *How to Make Things Out of Paper.* New York: Sterling Publishing Company, Inc., 1971. (Paper making activities, including Origami and paper games)

Tichenor, Tom. *Tom Tichenor's Puppets.* Nashville: Abingdon Press, 1971. (Designing and using puppets, and adapting stories)

Tobey, Kathrene M. *Learning and Teaching Through the Senses.* Philadelphia: Westminster Press, 1970. (Activities using all the senses)

Ward, Winfred. *Playmaking With Children: From Kindergarten Through Junior High School,* second ed. New York: Appleton-Century-Crofts, 1957. (Basic book in creative dramatics; includes lists of stories for acting out)
———————————. *Stories to Dramatize.* Anchorage, Kentucky: The Children's Theater Press, 1952. (An anthology)

Weiss, Harvey. *Collage and Construction.* New York: Young Scott Books, 1970. (Collage and construction as an art form)

Wilson, Erica. *Fun With Crewel Embroidery.* New York: Charles Scribner's Sons, 1965. (Stitchery)

Wiseman, Ann. *Making Things: The Hand Book of Creative Discovery.* Boston: Little, Brown and Company, 1973. (A collection of processes, using common materials in creative ways)

Wright, Kathryn S. *Let the Children Paint: Art in Religious Education.* New York: The Seabury Press, 1966. (A classic in painting experiences for children)

Young, Lois Horton. *Dimensions for Happening.* Valley Forge, Pa.: Judson Press, 1971. (Responses to Bible passages through the art media)

index

---

*Major headings are shown in capital letters.

124